GREASY BEND

Ode to a Mountain Road

By

Aaron McAlexander

Greasy Bend

Ode to A Mountain Road

ISBN-13 978-0-9854225-5-4

Third Printing

Printed in U.S.A.

Contents:

Contents continued:

Image courtesy of Marker History.Com

The view from Lovers Leap

Introduction to Fifty-Eight

Greasy Bend is long-gone, but anyone old enough to have driven up Lovers Leap Mountain on Highway 58 prior to the mid-1970's will surely remember that curve, along with the many other opportunities for excitement that crooked mountain road could provide.

Virginia is actually one of the smaller states, the thirty-seventh largest in the Union, but it can seem as big as Texas if you are driving across it on U.S. Route 58. Highway 58 crosses Virginia at its widest dimension, and although it may feel as though it is meandering all over the state, the road never actually strays more than a few miles from Virginia's southern border. The 508 mile length of United States Route 58 between Virginia Beach and Cumberland Gap makes it the longest United States Highway to be entirely contained within the borders of a single state.

U. S. Route 58 did not originate as a state-wide project, conceived by men of vision, engineered with precision, and designed to be a continuous highway from the Atlantic Ocean to Kentucky. The diverse parts of the road just kind of emerged from the ground, sprouting from a collection of older roads that were rerouted, regraded, and eventually connected to make Old Fifty-Eight a highway across the state.

Some segments of the highway emerged a lot later than others. Back around 1920, if someone wanted to travel from Stuart to Hillsville, the most direct route would have been to follow the Danville/Wytheville Pike. If the mode of travel was a horse drawn wagon, the traveler could have made the journey in about eight to twelve hours, depending on the weather and the load in the wagon. In dry weather, a traveler driving a Model-T might have made the journey in three hours or less. If the weather was bad and the road was muddy, making the trip in a Model-T could have taken all day.

The modest improvements that were made when that segment of the highway was declared to be a part of State Route 12 didn't reduce the expected travel time between Stuart and Hillsville that much, but the fact that the state began putting crushed stone on the road definitely increased the likelihood that either waggoneers or automobile drivers would be able to eventually complete the trip.

The real change in travel time between those two towns came following the completion of U.S. Route 58 in 1933, and the application of tar and gravel paving over its entire length. In the mid-1930's, a traveler could have expected to make the trip from Stuart to Hillsville in about an hour and a half. That was unless the weather was bad or the traveler got stuck behind a tractor-trailer near the foot of the mountain. In the 30's, it could take a big truck an hour to travel up Lovers Leap Mountain from Jim Hopkin's Store to Vesta, and there was no place in the mountain a truck could be pulled over to let cars by until it got to Lovers Leap.

Almost every part of old U.S. Route 58 has had its own special problems, and the most dangerous parts of the highway have not all been in the mountains.There used to be a stretch of Route 58 in the eastern part of the state between Cortland and Emporia, for example, that was given the unfortunate label of "Suicide Strip." Between 1970 and the conversion of that segment of the highway to four lanes in 1991, some 107 people lost their lives while traveling a 34 mile length of hill and dale road with few significant curves. Perhaps that is what prompted officials in the town of Emporia to establish such an efficient speed trap.

For the first fifty years of the highway's existence as U.S. Route 58, there were two mountainous sections that were dreaded by most folks, especially truckers, when they were traveling the western half of route. The section of the highway that passed near Whitetop Mountain in Grayson County was one of them, a narrow and curvy road that took you through an isolated area near the highest mountains in the state. The segment of Route 58 over Lovers Leap Mountain in Patrick County was not quite as isolated, but it was more heavily travelled and in some ways, more hazardous.

Folks who would drive the section of the highway that passed near Whitetop Mountain, between Volney and Damascus, used to refer to it as "going over Whitetop," and they avoided it if they could. A term like "Going over Whitetop" may sound pretty scary to anyone who is aware that Whitetop Mountain, at 5520 feet, is the second highest mountain in Virginia, but no part of US 58 has ever gone anywhere near the top of that mountain. The segment of Highway 58 that passes closest to the crest of Whitetop Mountain does pass near the town of Whitetop, Virginia, but only at an elevation of about 4000 feet. That segment of Route 58 follows what was once Virginia Highway 305, passing a few miles to the south of Whitetop Mountain, and even though it does not go over the top of Whitetop, it is still

35 miles of very crooked mountain road, varying between 2000 and 4000 feet in elevation.

County by county, as more of the problematic sections of U.S. Route 58 have been improved, hazards such as the two sections just mentioned, along with much of the highway between them, are at last being brought up to modern highway standards. The steel truss bridge across Snake Creek near Hillsville in Carroll County, for example, was known as a formidable highway hazard until it was replaced with a wider, curved bridge in the 1990's. The radius of the curve in which the bridge is located was also increased, greatly reducing one more serious hazard.

About midway in the short stretch of Route 58 that passes through the southern corner of Floyd County, there used to be a minor appearing bend that was known as "Dead Man's Curve." It acquired that name over 65 years ago as a result of a number of single vehicle accidents in just a few years, two of them fatal, followed by head-on crash in 1950 that killed five people. The curve really did not look to be that dangerous at all, and it really was just a minor twitch in the road for someone driving through it at the posted speed. There was this unexpected hump in the middle, however, where the elevation of the surface abruptly shifted from sloping toward the right side of the road to sloping toward the left, and that shift could cause a speeding car to veer into the opposing lane. That hazard was done away with when that section of Highway 58 from Meadows of Dan through Laurel Fork was upgraded to four lanes in 2015, at long last rendering "Dead Man's Curve" defunct.

It only takes a quick look at a Virginia roadmap to see that U.S. Route 58 is really two very different roads. Eastward from Stuart, the highway is entirely four lanes, and except for the convolutions required while following Route 58 through Portsmouth and Norfolk, it is a mostly linear thoroughfare. Immediately to the west of Stuart, however, the character of the road quickly changes. The two lane road winding up Lovers Leap Mountain for the first fifteen miles westward from Stuart serves as an introduction to a different class of highway. While there are some four lane segments that connect a few of the larger towns and bypass some communities, a majority of the mileage of U.S. Route 58 between Stuart and Cumberland Gap continues to be a meandering two-lane mountain road.

There appears to be considerable of political will for the completion of an all four-lane Highway 58 extending at least the distance from Norfolk westward to the intersection of Route 58 and I-77 just past Hillsville. Much of the impetus for such a project is the fact that Norfolk is one of the most important deep-water ports on the east coast, and one of only a few that will be able to handle the largest of the Chinese superfreighters that soon will be passing through the enlarged Panama Canal. The commercial advantages of having a direct four-lane connection for moving containerized freight from Norfolk to I-77 are obvious, but whether the value of such a project is worth the capital expenditure and the environmental impact is a subject that deserves some serious debate. Just a couple of years ago, a Virginia Representative assured me that a four lane Highway 58 up Lovers Leap Mountain will be completed within a decade. The recent collapse of the highway at several places on Lovers Leap Mountain due to heavy rains definitely adds credibility to the argument that some major improvements of the road are in order, but I

11

suspect that "Super 58" will actually be completed in some other decade.

Each section of United States Route 58 has its own history, and some of the many stories and legends associated with the segment of Highway 58 across Lovers Leap Mountain are a part of this book. It took two-thirds a century for the forty-some miles of the series of rutted and winding, dirt and gravel wagon roads that initially connected Stuart and Hillsville to be transformed into to one continuous county maintained road and designated as part of the Danville/Wytheville Pike. Later, "the pike" was made a part of the state maintained Virginia State Route 12. A few years later the road was further improved to become a narrow-but-paved section of U.S. Route 58 and eventually named the Jeb Stuart Highway. It is still a work in progress, thank goodness, continuing to be developed into a safer and smoother Route 58, complete with four-lane bypasses around Meadows of Dan and Laurel Fork.

Everyone with an awareness of history knows that the twentieth century was a time of incredible change, and there are none of those changes that have had a more profound effect on the lives of the people of rural America than the construction of the national highway system and its continual process of alteration and improvement.

Most significant change comes at a cost to someone, and the advent of the automobile and the development of highway systems to accommodate travel and commerce are no exception. In a short period of time, historically speaking, new roads have been built and old roads abandoned, then newer roads replaced, abandoned, or rerouted, over and over. Homes were destroyed and farm land was covered over with residential development, old businesses were ruined and new businesses were created, and many lives were disrupted by the relentless construction and alteration of our transportation routes. Sometimes folks, after having dwelled for generations in a pleasant rural environment, have found themselves living near a noisy transportation artery. Others, after having spent much of their lives beside a major highway, have ended up living by what has become a minor back road. Some folks were able to adapt to the change and to possibly even take advantage of it, while others hunkered down and dedicated the remainder of their lives to railing against those agencies responsible for the change.

I think that one of the best ways to appreciate the history of a particular period or place or culture is to learn stories about some of the people who actually lived it. This book is a collection of stories about people who were connected by one particular road, State Road 12/U.S. Highway 58. It is an accumulation of tales I have been told and even a few that I experienced myself, while living near a mountain highway that is a part of United States Route 58. My hope is that these stories will reveal something worthwhile about how that road has affected the lives of people who have lived near it and travelled over it for a period of more than a century.

These stories were all represented to me as being true, but some of the names, locations, and details have been altered for obvious reasons. The truth is the truth, some might say, but I will have to confess that some of these stories are truer than others.

If you are a Virginian who has never travelled the complete length of Route 58, maybe you should try it some time. Journeying along Highway 58 for long distances has always required concentrated effort and careful attention to avoid being led off onto some other route. I should warn you that, even today, when traveling the western segment of that highway, you will find it necessary to either ignore your GPS or to keep resetting it so that it only directs you from one mountain town to the next. If you set your GPS for the entire distance and follow the instructions given, it is certain that you will be directed along some highways far afield from Old Route 58. Your GPS might send you along interstates I-77 and I-81, or up U.S. Routes 16 and 11, possibly even directing you up through the coalfields of the state along ALT U.S. 58. There are other routes that can be taken from Virginia Beach to Cumberland Gap that require less time than adhering to Route 58, but there is no route between those extremities of the state that is fewer miles.

The GPS's diversions from the original Highway 58 allow for faster travel, it is true, but should you elect to take them, you will miss seeing some of the most interesting places. Besides, if you were in a really big hurry to get somewhere, you probably wouldn't be driving from Virginia Beach to Cumberland Gap in the first place.

In the Middle

"Oooo-kay everybody, is it Virginia Beach or Cumberland Gap that we're heading for today?"

That was Dad's tired old joke, the one we were sure to hear any time we were able to hound our dad into taking the family out for a Sunday afternoon drive. As he would reluctantly pull the old Dodge up to the top of our driveway and stop to cautiously check both ways before pulling out onto Route 58, he would always ask whether we were going to go to Virginia Beach or to Cumberland Gap on this trip.

Mom and my sisters would always cackle appreciatively, but I seemed to have missed the joke. When I finally asked Mom why she thought Dad's question was so funny, she explained that if we turned to the left out of the driveway and kept right on driving on Highway 58, we really could be at Cumberland Gap in about five hours. If we went to the right, we could possibly arrive in Virginia Beach in about the same amount of time. I had thought that Dad's query was supposed to be funny because our Sunday excursions rarely lasted more than hour, and they usually ended up at Grandma's house, about three miles away.

When I was a young kid, living with my family beside US Route 58 in Meadows of Dan, Virginia, I mostly just thought of that highway as the road that made it possible for Dad to drive us either westward to Hillsville or eastward to Stuart. But the Cumberland Gap versus Virginia Beach business made me curious enough to look up a map of Virginia in the Rand McNally Road Atlas in the school library. When I looked it up, there it was: The atlas clearly showed that

15

Meadows of Dan was located on a highway that ran continuously from one side of the state to the other. It was easy to see that the highway went all the way across Virginia at the state's greatest width and that the road never got very far from the southern border. But on the map, it did look like maybe we were a little closer to Cumberland Gap than we were to Virginia Beach.

The best I could figure, by adding up the distances the between all of the towns along Highway 58, the distance from Meadows of Dan to Virginia Beach was about 50 miles more than the distance from Meadows of Dan to Cumberland Gap. But I could tell, just by looking at the map, that a trip to Cumberland Gap along Highway 58 would require a lot of slow driving. Just looking in the atlas, anyone could see that Route 58 to the west was a very crooked road. But I figured that in terms of driving time, we probably were just about midway between the beginning and the end of U.S. Route 58 as it crossed the state of Virginia.

There seems to be an assumption that the people who live in small mountain communities are a long way out of the mainstream, but I don't recall feeling that way at all while growing up in Meadows of Dan. I may have been a bit naïve, but I really felt kind of in the middle of things, once I learned that I was living about midway between Virginia Beach and Cumberland Gap, and there's a way of thinking about the place that can make it seem really significant. In terms of travel time, Meadows of Dan, Virginia, is midway between the place where the first permanent English settlers waded ashore and into the new world in 1607 and the break in the Cumberland Mountains through which Daniel Boone led early settlers into Kentucky in 1775. I like to think of Old Highway 58 as a historical timeline.

16

The first time I ever saw the ocean, I was a young teenager who had just spent most of a long day riding the 275 mile distance to Virginia Beach on a school bus. That bus took us all the way from the Blue Ridge Mountains to the Virginia Shore without traveling a single mile on any highway other than on US Route 58. Traveling to the other end of the state, however, starting out on one of our rare trips to visit relatives who lived out west, I felt like the trip had not really begun until we had completed the two hundred miles it took to take us out of Virginia and into Kentucky. The last segment of Route 58, from Jonesville to Cumberland Gap, is known as the "Wilderness Road," and for good reason.

It is not just the location on U.S. Route 58 that keeps the mountain community of Meadows of Dan from being completely out of the mainstream either. Meadows of Dan happens to be located near milepost 177 on the Blue Ridge Parkway, one third of the length of the Parkway from its northern end near Waynesboro, Virginia. If you add in the 105 mile length of the Skyline Drive that runs through the Shenandoah National Park to the northern end, that puts Meadows of Dan just about midway between from the northern end at Front Royal, Virginia, and the southern terminus of the Blue ridge Parkway at Cherokee, North Carolina. It is also fortunate for Meadows of Dan that folks driving on the Blue Ridge Parkway are seldom in any great hurry, meaning that a lot of them will stop off for a visit. In fact, that may be one of the main reasons why Meadows of Dan can still be found on the map.

Driving the 508 mile distance from Virginia Beach to Cumberland Gap on United States Route 58 is a demanding trip even here in the twenty-first century, and there's no doubt but that it seemed even longer

17

back in the days when cars were less comfortable and there were more challenging aspects to the road. There are alternative routes that can be taken from Virginia Beach to Cumberland Gap that require significantly less time than following Route 58, of course, but there is no route between the extremes of the state that is fewer miles.

The official length of the highway today is a few miles less than it was back in 1932, when that series of older roads was first was cobbled together, paved, and given the "United States Route 58" designation. Much of what is now US 58 closely follows the path of old State Route 12, a mostly unpaved road that was established as a Virginia State Highway way back in 1918. State Route 12 originally provided a continuous route between Suffolk and Abingdon, and it made up about half of the total length of the road that eventually became U.S. Route 58. Before that, many parts of the roads that became Virginia State Route 12 were older roads that were in existence long before 1918. The section of Route 12 between Danville and Hillsville mostly followed the original *Danville/Wytheville Turnpike*, and that original "turnpike," was created from county roads that were first connected as far back as the 1850's, obviously to create a continuous route between Danville and Wytheville.

For years after State Route 12 had officially replaced the Danville/Wytheville Pike on the map, folks who lived near that road continued to refer to it as the Danville/Wytheville Pike. Even in the forties and fifties, years after the road had been officially christened United States Route 58, a lot of folks still referred it as "The Pike," in reference to its former status. It is interesting to note that the current name given to "58" from Hillsville eastward to the Patrick County line is the *Danville Pike*, and from Hillsville westward to Grayson County, it is named the *Carrolton Pike*.

There are a lot of stories about the early days of "Highway 58," that illustrate just how seriously some folks seem to have been attached to the idea of the Meadows of Dan/Laurel Fork area being central to the route between Danville and Wytheville, Virginia. My Grandpa McAlexander, who lived beside Highway 58 on the Patrick-Floyd County line, loved to tell a tale that is definitely a case in point.

It must have been something to see, that Saturday morning in 1935 when the big Packard Phaeton came speeding down the newly paved Route 58 from out of Floyd County and roaring into Patrick amid a cloud of dust and flying gravel. Just a couple of hundred yards into Patrick County, the driver of the Packard braked hard and veered the big car across the road, sliding to a stop in front of the gas pump at Taylor Cock's Store. That part of the country was still very much in the Great Depression at the time, and that automobile was the biggest, fanciest conveyance most of the men loafing around the store that morning had ever seen. Some of the loafers noted that the car was sitting rather low in the back, as if there might be a lot of extra weight hidden on the rear floorboard and in the trunk.

The driver of the car, a nattily dressed chap wearing a tweed jacket and a golf cap, leaned out over the top of the car door. "Fill'er up, he called out to the group of men standing around the front of the store, gaping. Denny, an employee of the store who was standing near the pump, shook off his amazement and began delivering fuel to the car. That took a little time, since he had to pump the ten-gallon glass tank at the top of the manual pump full three times before he finished filling up the fuel tank on that thirsty Packard. Like Denny told the others in the group around the store, the gas tank on that big-ole car must have been mighty close to empty, because it took over four dollars' worth of gasoline to fill it up!

The driver of the Packard politely declined the offer of an oil level and a tire pressure check, indicating that he was in a big hurry. "Keep the change," the driver told Denny, pressing a five dollar bill into his hand. But as he was pulling away from the pump, the driver suddenly braked the car to a stop, and leaning out over the car door he shouted back over his shoulder to Denny. "How much farther is it to Danville?"

Denny, took a couple of steps toward the car and, over the roar of the engine, yelled out the best information he could provide.

"Why, you're just about halfway there right now!" Denny shouted back to the driver.

*****

Back in the forties and fifties, Willie and Mollie Nelson [Not that Willie Nelson] ran a combination restaurant, store, and Texaco gas station beside the old route of Route 58 between Stuart and Martinsville. Its official name was the *Midway Service Station and Restaurant*, but most folks just referred to it as *Midway*. MIDWAY was painted in black letters two feet high on the side of the building, making it was something of a landmark on that sparsely populated section of highway. For folks who had driven all the way from Stuart to Martinsville for a movie some evening, Midway was a great place to stop and fill up the car, get something to eat, and maybe even pick up a loaf of bread on the drive back home. The business closed down after Highway 58 was rerouted so that the building no longer faced the main highway, but the old Midway building still stands.

Like almost everyone else, I thought that the name "Midway" came from the restaurant's location being midway between Stuart and Martinsville, and that probably is the case. But something clicked in my head as I drove past it a while back, and I decided to check and see if the name Midway had any broader implications. I checked out the distances using Google Earth®, and can you believe it? The old Midway Service Station is located midway between Virginia Beach and Cumberland Gap, I mean, to the nearest mile. The location of Old Midway, the building still standing at the western end of the road now known as Stella Loop, is at the midpoint of (Old) U.S. Route 58. Do you suppose that the owners were aware of that when they opened the place way back in 1939?

I'm thinking that the term "Midway" can be significant in some other ways as well. I'll bet that on any Saturday night back in the nifty fifties, there was not a dating couple in Meadows of Dan who was not acutely aware that they were located precisely midway between the Patrick Springs Drive-In Theater and the Hillsville Drive-In Theater, either of them just 20 miles away. Enough said about that.

*****

It should not be surprising that I should reminisce a bit about old Route 58, when you consider that most of the first eighteen years of my life was spent within a few yards of that highway. The house in which I was raised sat right beside that road, and almost everything I did and everywhere I went began with a trek along it. The highway passed right by the back of our house and ran along the top of an elevated embankment and was so close that we could distinctly hear all of the cars and trucks going by, even those that were traveling at normal highway speed. But the Big trucks and speeding cars would shake the windows in the walls and rattle the dishes in the cupboard when they passed. The sounds of traffic were so close in fact, if we were listening carefully, we could keep track of our neighbors' comings and goings, just from the sounds of their vehicles. Even the school building in which I received all twelve years of my public school education was located so close to that highway that it was hard to not be aware of the traffic much of the time, and the same thing was true for the church in which we attended services on most Sundays.

We tended our garden and hoed our corn in fields that were right beside Route 58. We milked our cows in a rickety old barn that would quiver with the blasts of air it received from passing cars and trucks. As we alternated the uses of our land, we would periodically have to brave the hazards of moving cows and hauling feed across that heavily travelled highway. We didn't think much about it at the time though, and most of our experiences were little different than those of the many other families who lived beside that long highway.

Every once in a while, usually about two or three o'clock in the morning, a vehicle would come blasting by so fast that we would all be jolted awake when the shock wave hit the house. It sometimes felt like the house was lifted off its foundation and given about a quarter of a turn, then dropped back to earth, as some powerful machine would roar on down 58, then quickly pass out of hearing range. The impact and noise would sometimes be so startling that I would sit straight up in bed and hear my sisters in the upstairs bedroom exclaiming, "What on earth was that?"

"That was probably Lionel Stanley trying out a new racing engine," Dad would grump up at them from downstairs. "Now go back to sleep."

Lionel Stanley was a local automotive wizard known for the high-performance engines he built for racing cars and some other purposes. He built the engines in his shop beside U.S. 58 in Patrick near the Floyd County line before he began building them for Holman-Moody Racing in Charlotte.

*****

In the summers when I was a kid, I used to sometimes spend the night with cousins who lived right beside Route 58 where it weaved its crooked path through uptown Stuart. Sometimes, when the nights were very hot, the windows of the house would be kept open. That improved the temperature inside the house, of course, but the trucks passing through town on the highway would often keep us from sleeping. Instead of counting sheep, my cousins and I would count the number of times a truck would have its gears shifted as it passed through the town. From the time we could first hear a trailer-truck topping the big hill to the east of Stuart, we would follow the truck by its sound, as it accelerated down that hill, then groaned across the creek, through the curves up the next hill, and passed on into town. It would slowly weave through the town, up the hill past the Ford Place and Main Street, on out to West End, then finally rev down the long hill past Paul's Place, cross the Mayo River and pass out of hearing. The number of gear shifts counted usually fell between sixty and seventy, but I recall the record number of shifts we counted from a single truck passing through Stuart as being one hundred and four.

Please understand that I am not comparing myself to Mark Twain or anything like that, but when I was a kid, I really did love reading his books. Tom Sawyer and Huckleberry Finn were among my favorites, but Twain's book that fascinated me the most was his *Life on the Mississippi.* It was impossible for a young boy growing up in the Blue Ridge Mountains of Virginia to have any real understanding of what life might have been like for someone his own age who lived through his formative years on the banks of the mile-wide Mississippi River, but that does not mean I did not try.

My childhood years were spent on the banks of Tuggles Creek, a pitiful little branch that I could jump across, a stream that not even the most creative imagination could connect to the Mighty Mississippi. My substitute for the Big River was United States Route 58. That may seem strange, but consider this: Everywhere I went, nearby or far away, the journey was begun by going up the drive and turning one way or the other onto Highway 58. That was the case whether I was walking the quarter of a mile up the hill to the general store, or leaving with my family on the three day journey to visit my Aunt in Iowa. To my young unacculturated mind, United States Route 58 was the artery of commerce that connected Meadows of Dan with the rest of the world, vaguely in the same way that Mark Twain described the connection of Hannibal, Missouri that was provided by the Mississippi River. So far as I could tell, everything anyone in our community might buy, rent, borrow, or sell came onto or went out from their homes and farms via Route 58.

During World War II and for several years afterwards, if folks living near Highway 58 needed to go to town, even if they had used all their gasoline ration stamps or they did not have a car, there was no problem. There were two busses a day that passed through in either direction, and they would take you as far west as Galax or as far east as Danville, Virginia. All you had to do was to walk out to the highway before the bus came by and wave it down as it approached. And from those towns just mentioned, you could connect with other busses that could take you anywhere in the country you might want to go.

Anyone who does not live on an island has to live near a street, a highway, or at least a country lane. In our world today, one's connection to the rest of the world is really just a matter of how many turns one is willing to take while getting wherever it is they are trying to go. And almost sixty years after I moved away from it, I continue to harbor a special attachment to that long, long road known as Highway 58, the artery of commerce that, at least in my own mind, connected Meadows of Dan to the world. While Mark Twain may have written about dreaming of becoming a river boat pilot, I used to think about how what an exciting life it must be, driving the bus between Galax and Danville.

Spending all those years in the shadow of US 58 has to have had its effect, especially when one considers the many hazards of living right beside such busy highway. Bruce Thomas, a young cousin of mine, was killed while riding his bicycle on that road. Not nearly as tragic, but sad none the less, my first two puppies met their end on Highway 58, and a large but uncounted number of family cats met a similar fate.

As I get along in years and more and more frequently can't recall a name or remember where I left my reading glasses, I worry if maybe all those years of breathing the exhaust fumes from passing vehicles powered by leaded gasoline has affected my brain.

Greasy Bend

Lovers Leap Mountain, that well-known section of US Route 58 between Meadows of Dan and Stuart, may not be made into four lanes for a few years to come, but even now it is nothing like the truckers' nemesis that it was not so many years ago. Today, there is an average casualty rate of perhaps one trucking accident every couple of months, as compared to a rate of about one truck per week prior to the major improvements that were made in the seventies. The most significant of those improvements has to have been the elimination of the infamous curve known as *Greasy Bend*. For many years, about half of the trucks that wrecked while traveling down that mountain either went out of control in Greasy Bend or a little farther down the road, in either the Bob Fain Curve or the Harley Hopkins Curve.

The stream of commuters that now travels up and down Lover's Leap Mountain in the mornings and evenings is just a fraction of what it used to be. Like so many other parts of the country, most of the factories in southwestern Virginia towns such as Stuart, Martinsville, and Bassett are now closed and the jobs they once provided for the people in the region have been moved offshore to Asia. For many years though, every weekday morning and evening, there would be a stream of workers commuting up and down that mountainous section of Route 58 between Meadows of Dan and the towns in the piedmont below. For a few decades though, many mountain folks felt they were enjoying the best of all possible worlds; they could continue to live in the mountains they loved and commute from there to decent jobs in town.

Over the period during which so many mountain road commuters were traveling Lovers Leap Mountain, names were given to every significant curve encountered during that drive. Most of the curves were given the names of the folks whose homes were close by. Just like a lot of the old farms in the area, those bends continue to be known by the names of the citizens who once lived there, even though most of the people for whom they were named have long since departed from this world.

It is still a little hard for me to comprehend the four-lane alternate routes that have recently been built around communities such as Laurel Fork and Meadows of Dan, Virginia, but on the other hand, most of the towns and communities that lie along Highway 58 to the east of Stuart have long been bypassed. The original Route of 58 as it passed through "downtown" Meadows of Dan was never all that curvy, but the bypass has definitely improved traffic safety near the elementary school and the stores in Meadows of Dan, and especially near the intersection of Highway 58 with the Blue Ridge Parkway.

If you are not from the area but you want to fully appreciate the obstacle that Lovers Leap Mountain presents to efficiently connecting the Atlantic seaport at Norfolk to I-77 via U.S. Route 58, maybe you should take the scenic drive along Route 58 from Meadows of Dan to Stuart. It is only a short distance after leaving the bypass and heading east out of Meadows of Dan before some of the limitations imposed by this two lane section of the highway begin to become clear.

Just after passing the post office and the bank, the first major crooked road hazard is encountered, a complicated curve called the Tump Spangler Bend. That combination of curves has been known by that name since the early 1930's, and it is a bend in the road with a lot of unfortunate history. One of the most horrific tragedies ever to occur in the community of Meadows of Dan was a head-on collision in the Tump Spangler Bend that took the lives of a young couple, Jesse and Alva Harrell and the life of Alva Harrell's mother. In May of 1939, as Jesse Harrell was driving westward through that curve, his car was struck head-on by a truck traveling on the wrong side of the road at a high speed. Mr. Harrell was driving a Model-A Ford, a car that had its gasoline tank located under the cowling just in front of the windshield. The collision caused the car to explode into flames, fatally burning all three of the car's occupants and making orphans of the Harrell's four young children. Jesse Harrell's brother Dorsey and Alva Harrell's sister Clara were a married couple with four children of their own, but Dorsey and Clara immediately took in the deceased couple's four children. The story of Dorsey and Clara Harrell so successfully raising their expanded family of eight children on their farm in Meadows of Dan has been an inspiration to the community for generations.

Even while making the short trek from Meadows of Dan to the top of the mountain, you will need to be wary of the Dewey Wood Curve, the Edgar Cassell Curve, and several others. But now, just as it was back in the day, the real excitement of driving down Lovers Leap Mountain begins about a mile to the east of Vesta, shortly after negotiating the Henry Cassell Curve and cresting at the "top of the mountain." The "Top of The Mountain" is the unofficial name for the beginning point of the descent down Lover's Leap Mountain to the foot hills, and it is marked by a sign that says "Elevation: 3000 ft." For anyone making that trip down the mountain for the first time, it is helpful to be aware that the road descends some 1500 feet in six miles and that the grade sometimes exceeds nine percent. Although many of the worst curves have been improved or eliminated, and others have been widened and modified, the average grade down the mountain has not been significantly changed since its initial construction. Before some significant improvements were made, both in the highway and in the vehicles descending it, there were about twenty curves in that mountain road that had the potential to create havoc for the unskilled or the inattentive driver, especially in times of severe winter weather. There is also a short list of the curves in that mountain that have created more difficulty than all of the others combined, especially for the big trucks.

After leaving "the top of the mountain" and heading toward Stuart, the first curve encountered is called the Woolwine Curve by some, alluding to the possibility that trying to go around that curve too fast can result in one taking a shortcut to Woolwine, a community at the foot of the mountain about 1200 feet below. Others call it the "Rock House Curve" because of the rock house that stands on a bluff across the valley to the north side of the curve. (The rock house can only be seen in the winter when the trees are bare, but you need to keep your eyes on the road anyway.)

The next curve goes by the Birdhouse Store, a business structure that was known for many years as Lover's Leap Tavern. It has not been too many years since a tractor-trailer turned over onto the inside of that curve and spilled out several tons of peanuts onto the shoulder. Shortly after that accident, the county prudently put up the "Bear Crossing" sign that you may notice as you approach the curve.

Note: Back when the Birdhouse Store was still a tavern, the uniformity of the centerline, always repainted from the bottom to the top of the mountain, was much more consistent as it approached the tavern than it became just after passing it. Go figure.

Following the curve that goes by the tavern, there is a half-mile stretch of road with a slight uphill grade that zig-zags past Lover's Leap Wayside (AKA, The Rock Cut). This landmark is readily identifiable by the rock wall to the left which has a spectacular view beyond it and the initials of hundreds of imbeciles spray painted all over it. This short, slightly uphill section can give truckers an opportunity to cool their brakes and possibly gear down a couple more notches before starting the big descent.

After "The Leap," as the entire first mile of the descent from the top of the mountain is sometimes known, comes a broad s-curve that has plenty of shoulder room making it easy to negotiate (that was not always the case), but from there, it is literally downhill for the next five miles, beginning with a mile of steep downhill chicanes. The names of many of the curves in the mountain are not as well-known as they once were, but I can recall either seeing, reading, or hearing about an accident in just about every one of them. That's not including the uncounted number of wrecks caused by snowy or icy conditions that those involved considered too minor to be reported.

A hazard that has long been associated with Lovers Leap Mountain (and the Blue Ridge Mountains in general) is really serious fog. One simple improvement was the obvious safety measure of painting the center line of the road yellow and marking the shoulders of the road with white lines. Those lines on the shoulders make it much, much easier to negotiate any crooked road in the fog, but this was not done along Route 58 in Lovers Leap Mountain until the 1970's. There are many stories about how hazardous the fog on Lovers Leap Mountain can be. I can remember one of them especially well, since it involved my aunt.

Early on one very foggy morning in the late 1940's, Mrs. Fanny Thomas was driving down the mountain to her job as a nurse in the office of Dr. W.N. Thompson in Stuart. She was just above the bend then known as the Johnny Williams Curve (it is called the Midkiff Curve today), when the fog became so thick that she completely lost sight of the road. In the morning darkness, she drove her car off the road and over the shoulder, crashing down the mountain side. This was before cars had seat belts, but Mrs. Thomas was somehow able to retain her seat inside the car as it rolled down the mountainside, completely turning over at least twice. She said that she just hung on to the steering wheel and prayed until the car came to a stop, miraculously landing upright on its wheels.

As she was gathering her thoughts, wondering if anyone would ever find her there and if she should try to climb back up the mountainside to the road, she realized that her car was sitting almost level and that the engine was still running. She then realized that the car had landed upright in a part of what had once been old State Route 12, the predecessor of U.S. 58, and the old road where the car stopped was still passable because it still served as an access road to a couple of homes. Mrs. Thomas was able to drive her battered but still mobile '41 Chevrolet the short distance out to

Highway 58, where she flagged down another commuter who took her to her doctor's office in Stuart. Except for some minor bumps and bruises, she was not injured, but she really did not feel like working that day. As an employee from the office drove Mrs. Thomas back up the mountain to her home, they stopped to look at her car. There it sat beside the road, scratched, battered, and missing half of the windshield, with the engine still idling like a sewing machine.

Once you have successfully negotiated the Midkiff Curve on your trip down Lovers Leap Mountain, you will have made it about half-way. For the first forty years or so, the main obstacles to a successful completion of the descent from that curve on down would have been, in the order in which they were encountered, the Green Martin Curve, Greasy Bend, the Bob Fain Curve, and the Harley Hopkins Curve.

There's a lot more that can be said about those bends in the road, especially Greasy Bend. Before the improvements in the 1970's, by the time a vehicle going down the mountain was approaching Greasy Bend, there was less than a mile to go before the road leveled out at the foot of the mountain. But after having negotiated most of the steep and twisting road down the mountain, drivers would suddenly come upon this very tight, decreasing radius right-hand turn of 180 degrees. That was sometimes a big problem for a heavily loaded truck that had gained too much speed and had brakes that were already burning.

One retired semi-trailer driver told me about a harrowing descent he once made down that last stretch of the mountain. He said that he knew he was in trouble when he found that his truck, heavily loaded with

33

machine tools, was just barely to make it around the Midkiff Curve. He was able to keep his rig in the road as he exited that curve, and struggled for the next mile, as he faced the series of chicanes followed by the swooping double-s called the Green Martin Curve. He knew the road well enough to realize that the next curve he was going to have to deal with was Greasy Bend. His brakes had been roiling smoke since the Midkiff curve, so he chose to put his right-hand wheels into the ditch and let the trailer scrub up against the road bank. He drove in the side ditch all the way around the curve and down the straight from Greasy Bend, almost to the Bob Fain Curve, before the truck finally came to a stop. He tore up the trailer pretty good, he said, but at least he survived, and the tractor and the load were salvageable. He was thankful that the accident happened late at night and he did not meet another vehicle between the Midkiff Curve and Greasy Bend.

Both Greasy Bend and the Bob Fain Curve were eliminated from Highway 58 about forty years ago, the sharply curved segments replaced by a continuous longer and less steeply inclined downhill straight in a different direction. The replacement section has two emergency escape ramps, one just before the straight and one about halfway down. Before they were eliminated, however, the one-two combination of Greasy Bend and the Bob Fain Curve took out more trucks than all of the other bends in the mountain combined. In the worst case scenario, a truck that was really rolling as it approached Greasy Bend might never really get into the sharpest part of the curve, but would go up and over the slight embankment on the outside at the beginning of the curve instead, heading over the side of the mountain and into oblivion. Sometimes, a truck

34

would jackknife midway through the curve, then flip over and slide across the road to the outside of the turn, possibly even sliding on over the side of the mountain further down. But drivers who were familiar enough with the curve to put their right-hand wheels in the ditch and slow their rigs by scraping out the trailer's undercarriage said it beat the alternative. Some claim that was no worse than using a poorly maintained escape ramp.

If a driver who approached Greasy Bend too fast still managed to guide the rig around that troublesome curve, then he or she would quickly become aware of the second part of the double whammy. Exiting Greasy Bend and heading on down the mountain was a straight shot down a thirteen percent grade that led to an abrupt 180 degree turn to the left. That curve had a posted maximum safe speed of 25 mph back them, and the sign wasn't kidding. It was known as the Bob Fain Curve, and there was even a saying about it. "If Greasy Bend don't get you, Bob Fain just might."

If a truck driver charging down Lovers Leap Mountain got through the Bob Fain curve, then he almost had it made, but not necessarily. Barring something really unexpected, it could now be clear sailing all the way to Norfolk, but the unexpected was often there, just waiting. Sometimes a driver would feel overconfident upon exiting the Bob Fain curve and let'er roll too soon, only to be done in by the seemingly minor Harley Hopkins Curve, about a mile farther down the road. The road may have appeared to have leveled out, but that was simply in comparison to the road just travelled. The "level out" at the foot of the mountain still had a significant two to three degree grade, enough to cause a truck with brakes that were seriously

35

overheated to continue to accelerate. If you drive down that mountain today, you just might notice the unusual warning sign put beside the road to notify truckers of the deceptive Harley Hopkins Curve, 1000 feet ahead. The sign is on the right, just past the intersection of Route 58 and Trot Valley Road.

My dad drove to and from his job with the Virginia Department of Highways, going up and down Lover's Leap Mountain many times a week for over thirty years. It seemed like he would come home with a report of an accident in the mountain at least once a month, and more often than not, it was a wreck that had happened in Greasy Bend.

It was about 1940 that the most famous of all of the big wrecks happened in that curve. A refrigerated tractor-trailer owned by the Armour-Star Company, fully loaded with meat products of course, turned over onto the outside lane of the bend. The trailer split wide open, scattering hams, shoulders, and sides of bacon all through the curve. Word soon got around, and with the hot summer weather making the meat sure to spoil anyway, folks from all around there thought it was their duty to help clean up the mess. Almost all of the meat that spilled out into the road had vanished within a couple of hours. Dad said he was waiting in the backed-up traffic when he saw a little kid latch onto a ham that was too big for him to move. Then, some helpful person tied a piece of rope onto the ham, and the last my dad saw of the kid, he was dragging it down the side of the road toward the foot of the mountain.

By the time the wrecker arrived, there was not a scrap of meat to be found anywhere, and once the wreck had been hauled away, the only indication there was ever an accident in the bend was a lot of grease smeared all over the road. Some said that it could have been even worse, had not all of the meat been so quickly removed from the road by the conscientious citizenry. There was still so much grease left on the road following the wreck that the curve was even more of a hazard for weeks, and that was obviously enough to give the curve its enduring name of *Greasy Bend*.

The descriptive name of the curve was reinforced about thirty years later when a tractor-trailer loaded with cases of motor oil turned over in Greasy Bend and spilled the cargo all over the road. Although some cans of oil burst open and spilled their contents throughout the curve, many cases of the oil remained salvageable. It took some time to get a heavy-duty wrecker and another company truck to the site, so a fellow was hired to oversee the wreckage overnight. By the next morning, however, most of the salvageable cargo had vanished. Now, I'm normally not suspicious natured, but the fellow who was supposed to be guarding the wreck did just happen to own a service station.

I'm not quite old enough to remember the wreck that originally gave Greasy Bend its name, but that big wreck was just one of the early ones, and there were many more to come. I can recall the spring morning when a trailer brimming full with a bulk load of seed corn turned over onto the upper side of Greasy Bend and slid through the curve, spilling out corn all over the road and onto both shoulders. Most of the corn was removed, of course, but enough was left distributed along on both sides of the road that the bountiful corn crop that grew beside the road the following summer made the curve look like it was winding through a bamboo forest. One of the local farmers was so impressed with the Greasy Bend corn crop that he called the state highway department to see if they knew what variety of seed corn the truck had been carrying.

While on their way to work early one very foggy morning, Dad and another state worker, Harry Spangler, fell in behind a truck that looked like it had a loose tarp flapping in the back. Peering at the back of the truck through the fog, they then realized that what they had first thought to be a flapping tarp was actually the trunk of an elephant, swinging out over the tailgate of a circus truck. As the truck was heading into greasy bend, the fog suddenly became so thick that the driver had to brake really hard. The quick braking caused the elephants to stagger to the lower side of the truck, definitely a serious case of the load shifting. The suspension of the truck apparently collapsed, causing it to veer into the ditch on the inside of the curve. The truck stopped leaning over against the bank, but it was going slowly enough that not a single one of the pachyderms was injured. While Dad helped the guys from the truck get the animals out and moved away from the wreck, Harry went up the road to put out some flares. But he was too late. Just moments after the elephants had been unloaded and moved to safety, a truckload of vitreous china bathroom fixtures came smoking down the mountain through the fog. The driver of the bathroom fixture truck managed to avoid hitting the circus truck, but his truck jackknifed and turned over, scattering and shattering sinks and commodes all over the highway. Fortunately, no one was hurt. Dad said he even tried to make some kind of joke out of that combination of wrecks, but was never able to come up with anything that was the least bit funny.

Just a couple of years before the road was upgraded and Greasy Bend blessedly eliminated, an auto transporter loaded with new cars lost its brakes back up in the mountain somewhere, and the rig was going so fast by the time it got to Greasy Bend that it hardly even got into the curve itself. The transporter just went straight across the road and up the embankment, crashing through the guard rail and rolling down the side of the mountain, scattering new Chevrolets as it went.

A couple of days later, after all of the wreckage of the cars and the transporter had been cleared, the Highway Department sent a crew up to Greasy Bend to replace the torn-out sections of the guard rail. That crew had worked all day, detaching the bent-up steel railings and loading them onto a truck, then digging out the sheared-off posts, and finally tamping in new posts and bolting new railings into place. It was just before quitting time and they were tightening the last bolts on the shiny new guard rail, when they heard a truck's brakes screeching through the Green Martin curve, just a little ways up the mountain.

Cruise Howell, one of the workmen who had just been replacing the guard rail, vividly described the accident. "We could tell that truck was comin' way too fast. We could hear the brakes a'squalling when it was way back up the road and they were so on fire we could smell the truck even before we could see it. We knew it was not going to make it around Greasy Bend and the only thing for us to do was to shag off down the side of the mountain." A truck load of apples plowed straight through the new sections of guard rail that the state workmen had just finished putting in place. Neither of the men replacing the railing nor the driver of the truck were injured, and the apples were reported to have been pretty good as well.

But neither Greasy Bend nor the Bob Fain Curve is a part of Route 58 anymore. Fifty-eight down Lovers Leap Mountain, all the way from the Midkiff Curve to Jim Hopkin's Store was rebuilt in the seventies. The Green Martin Curve has been straightened out considerably, and the combination of Greasy Bend and the Bob Fain Curve has been completely replaced with a long straight stretch leading down that last part of the mountain almost to the Mayo River.

There does remain a section of old Highway 58 that can be accessed by turning onto Trot Valley Road, right next to the Old Hopkin's Store (now a real estate business). Some folks occasionally drive the couple of miles up "Old 58," a segment of road that has been renamed Greasy Bend Lane in remembrance. I recently drove up that lane and around the old Bob Fain Curve (it seems even worse now than I remembered) and on up the steep straight to the lower end of Greasy Bend. Most of the famous old curve is now buried under its much improved replacement, but you can use Google Earth to zoom in onto that part of Route 58, and see the image of old Greasy Bend's original route passing underneath the present highway.

There is no question but that the road down Lover's Leap Mountain is just a whole lot safer today than it used to be, but the reduction in the number of trucking accidents is not just due to improvements in the road. I have been told that a lot of the reduction is because almost all large diesel truck engines are now equipped with compression release engine brakes (AKA, *Jake Brakes*). I've even heard it said that if those engine brakes had been around years ago, Greasy Bend might never have become so well known. Computerized braking systems also may help drivers maintain control of their trucks in emergency situations, and GPS technology has made extreme curves such as Greasy Bend and the Bob Fain Curve less of a surprise to drivers who are unfamiliar with the road. I've also been told that there is an important difference in the quality and the amount of rubber tread that trucks have in contact with the road these days, compared to the trucks of the 1930's and 40's. Back then, many tractor-trailer rigs were 10-wheelers or 14-wheelers instead of the 18-wheelers and more that most of them are today.

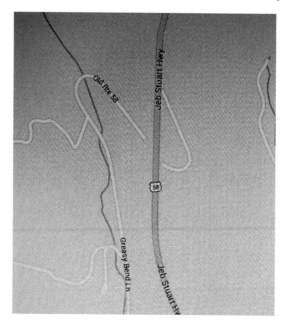

Google Earth displays the original route of Greasy Bend passing underneath current Route 58.

Resurrection

"♫ Go tell Aunt Rhody, go tell Aunt Rhody, go tell Aunt Rhody, the old gray goose is dead." It was just a silly children's song, but Rhoda would seethe inside every time she heard her younger sisters sing it.

Rhoda was a mountain farm woman, raised on the principles of piety and hard work and blessed with much too much common sense to allow herself to be swayed by worldly concerns such as vanity or pride. Her Primitive Baptist Faith had taught her that true happiness is not to be found in this life and that modesty and resolution reap their own true rewards, but Lord have mercy, how she hated that song.

Rhoda had passively observed as each of her two older sisters were courted by suitable suitors, both of them becoming betrothed and married within a period of a couple of years. She had just naturally assumed that her time would come, but now more years had passed her by, and still no one she might give any serious consideration had come courting. It hadn't worried her so much when her older sisters got married, but when her younger sister Fannie was sought out and married to a well-to-do widower from Meadows of Dan, Rhoda began struggling with feelings of rejection and exclusion.

Rhoda became especially sensitive to her situation when people she knew started calling her "Aunt Rhody." Folks who were her own age and older, some who were not even related to her began to call her "Aunt," making it a title she detested. No one meant to be hurtful or to imply anything derogatory by calling her "Aunt Rhody," and the nickname doubtlessly came from the traditional song that just about everyone knew at that time. Mountain people have never been very thoughtful about the nicknames with which they might burden their friends and family, but Rhoda just assumed hers had been given just because it was so obvious to everyone that she was on her way to becoming a spinster.

All of the sisters in that family were "big boned" women, as they used to say, but Rhoda was endowed with an especially sturdy frame. She was broad shouldered and nearly six feet tall, and so strong that folks said she could outwork most men. She had sometimes been described as a "handsome" woman while in her youth, but in adulthood, her size and strength, and even her coarse voice made her intimidating to many men. As she aged into her twenties and remained unmarried, Rhoda began to wonder if there was any man alive who could love a woman who wore a size thirteen shoe.

Then came the Sunday when she was attending the Annual Primitive Baptist Association Meeting and her older sister Elizabeth came sidling up, leading a strange man by the arm. She introduced the slender, leathery gentleman as her neighbor Wilshire, and quickly added that he had, unfortunately, lost his wife just this past December.

Rhoda grasped his hand and expressed her sincere condolences, while Wilshire stammered his appreciation for her concern and his leathery face turned crimson. After Elizabeth skittered off and left the two standing uncomfortably together, they first exchanged obligatory comments on the weather and the meeting before Wilshire began to show some moderate interest. He asked some serious questions about her family and her faith and then asked her if she would mind calling him Wil. Later that same day, not long after tasting her biscuits and fried chicken at the Association's "dinner on the grounds," he sought her out and asked if he could come a-courting.

Chemistry was not a word that would have been used to describe an instant attraction between two people in that time and place, but with Wilshire and Rhoda, there was definitely an immediate interest from both parties. In any case, there were few competing options for either of them, and the fact that Rhody was almost a head taller than Wilshire seemed not to matter to either of them in the least. The courtship that began soon led to a proposal with an immediate acceptance. Prompt plans for a quiet wedding were made, all within the span of a couple of months. As she and her sisters were planning for the wedding, however, Rhoda did confide that she thought she might have been selected by Wilshire on an entirely practical basis. "Why Fanny, she confided to her younger sister, Wil acts like getting married is like buying a horse or something. He just wants to get hitched up with a wife who's strong and good natured and can work like a mule. I'll be surprised if he don't pry my mouth open to look at my teeth before the wedding." Rhoda and her sisters would chuckle over that private joke on many occasions in the years to come.

In the years that followed her marriage to Wilshire, Rhoda began to experience a true sense of affirmation. Wilshire's white clapboard farm house near Laurel Fork was large and comfortable by the standards of the day, and his farm was one of the most prosperous around. The farm was located on the Dugspur Road, a location Rhoda considered to be most fortuitous. Not only did the road provide ready access to the outside world, at least by turn-of-the-century, Eastern Appalachian standards, but it enabled her to keep up with the comings and goings of the neighbors. If there was any gossip in the air, those neighbors could be depended upon to stop by and share it. The nearest thing to happiness Rhoda had ever known was living on that farm, raising her large family, and working in the fields every daylight hour that she was not busy inside the house, cooking, cleaning, and caring for the children. And with a dozen nieces and nephews living in the area, the nickname "Aunt Rhody" even became something of a title of honor to her.

Laurel Fork, Virginia, came into existence because of the intersection of the two main roads through the area, the Dugspur Road running in a generally north-south direction, and the Danville/Wytheville Turnpike, which basically ran east and west. The "Pike," as most folks called it, was a cobbled together series of country lanes that also happened to connect the community of Meadows of Dan, Virginia to the village of Laurel Fork.

It was rather pretentious of the state to designate that road as a turnpike, considering that it was really just a dirt wagon road winding across the Appalachian highlands. The term "turnpike" was then associated with any road that was constructed and maintained by the state, although a few years earlier, the term "pike" meant that one had to pay a toll to use the road. This "pike" was a free public road, mostly of single wagon width, and it was state maintained. That only meant that crushed stone was sometimes sparingly applied to the worst mud holes following the spring thaw.

Around 1906, however, word spread through Laurel Fork that "the pike" was going to undergo some major improvements. Not only was much of the road to be rerouted, but now the steepest climbs would be graded, and most of the larger streams would be bridged. The Danville-Wytheville Pike was to become a part of a state road that would run all the way from Abingdon to Suffolk.

Rhoda was indifferent when Wil began telling her about the "pike" being upgraded, but that was before she learned that the new road would pass farther from their home in Laurel Fork. Then her sister Fannie began smugly chatting about how the new route of the pike would be passing right by her home in Meadows of Dan. Rhoda felt a precipitous drop in status, now that that she and Wilshire were being "by-passed." Sister Fanny would now be the one with the nearest access to the outside world and the one to hear the gossip first. Rhody was a good Christian woman who knew that pride and envy were wrong. She was too practical and too busy to outwardly reveal such feelings to anyone, but she still could not help how she felt.

Rhoda continued her life as an Appalachian farm woman who was consistently stoic and uncomplaining. She was so stoic, in fact, that when she awoke Wilshire in the early hours of one cold March morning to tell him that she was sick   really, really sick   Wilshire did not question or hesitate to take action. He first suggested that he go get the doctor, but Rhoda's pain became so intense he decided that it might take too much time to get the doctor back to their home.

Wilshire woke the oldest daughter, Annabelle, and instructed her to gather up some quilts and make a pallet in the wagon while he hitched up the team. After instructing the young ones about how they were to look after the animals and each other, they laid Rhoda on her back in the farm wagon and drove out into the early morning darkness and onto the Dugspur Road. A short distance later they turned out onto the pike.

Wilshire guided the team and Annabelle tried to brace Rhody against the jolting and rocking of the wagon as they made their way along the rutted, frozen road. In spite of Annabelle's best efforts, Rhody responded to the many bumps with grunts and moans, creating for Wilshire the dilemma between the need for haste and the desire to avoid causing her any more pain.

Dr. Branscomb, the only physician within a radius of several miles, was accustomed to seeing patients at all hours of the day or night. He had heard the wagon coming up the lane and was opening the door to his home and office before Wilshire had even knocked. The doctor's wife, also his assistant, held up a bright "Aladdin" kerosene lamp while Wilshire and the doctor helped Rhoda into the doctor's parlor, also his examination room. The doctor wasted no time in proceeding with the examination.

As Rhoda indicated the location of the pain in her abdomen to Dr. Branscomb, his poking and prodding elicited shrieks of pain such as Wilshire had never heard from her, other than when she was giving birth. Rhoda's fever was running so high that the doctor gave her a dose of quinine to prevent convulsions, and the combination of abdominal pain and high fever prompted him to pronounce a diagnosis that was simple and direct: Rhoda had acute appendicitis with immediate surgery required. When Wilshire said that he thought perhaps it would be better if they tried to get Rhoda to a hospital, the doctor was more relieved than offended. He did not have a real operating room, and more than one of his appendectomies had resulted in the patients' succumbing to secondary infection. The doctor's dining room table was a location for surgery where aseptic conditions were difficult to maintain.

Dr. Branscomb even suggested that with the roads being so bad, perhaps they should take Rhoda to the hospital at Christiansburg. The fastest and least painful means of getting Rhoda there would be to take the railroad from the Betty Baker Mine at Sylvatus, rather than subjecting her to the agonies of wagon travel all the way. He didn't hold out much hope for Rhoda either way, the doctor admitted to Wilshire, as quietly and as gently as he could. He did send them on their way with a generous bottle of laudanum, a tincture of alcohol and opium which would make the trip to Christiansburg less painful for Rhoda, and possibly ease her journey into the next world.

The trip to Sylvatus was twenty more miles of rutted and frozen mountain road, a wearisome trip for Wilshire and Annabelle and truly an agonizing ordeal for Rhoda. They arrived at the Betty Baker Station in the early afternoon, allowing Wil just enough time to find someone to look after his horses and for him and Anabelle to get Rhoda and her pallet bundled on board the train. The few passengers already seated on the benches that ran along either side of the interior of the small passenger car helpfully squeezed together to make room for Rhoda's pallet of quilts to be rolled out on the floor with Wilshire and Annabelle seated on either side to assist and comfort her. The single wooden passenger car was attached like an afterthought to the end of a train made up of several hopper cars filled with copper ore and a few stock cars loaded with odd assortments of sheep, cattle, and hogs.

The Betty Baker Train was a "dead-ender," running on a narrow-gauge track originally built to haul away the ore dug from the Betty Baker Copper Mine. But the railway was also used to transport passengers, lumber, livestock, and anything else that needed to be shipped into or out of Carroll County, Virginia in the second decade of the twentieth century. There was no turnstile at the end of the line at Sylvatus; the little steam engine would back empty cars into the rail yard at Betty Baker, shuffle back and forth along the tracks, and eventually pull a string of loaded cars back out.

Almost as soon as the train had begun to slowly pull away from the yard, Wilshire realized that the train was a means of travel much preferable to a horse drawn wagon. The train may have rocked and jerked, but the motion was much less painful for Rhoda than riding in a jolting wagon. The laudanum may have been responsible, but when Rhoda told Wilshire that her pain had gotten better, he knew that was not necessarily a hopeful sign.

Having been up for much of the night before, Wilshire and Annabelle were hoping to sleep through some of the two-hour trip to Christiansburg, but as the train picked up speed and the car began to pitch and yaw around the mountain curves, they both were beset by the nausea and vertigo of their first ever experiences with motion sickness. A sympathetic fellow passenger who had been watching them care for Rhoda suggested that perhaps the medicine they were giving her might also be good for motion sickness. They had no idea what a proper dose would be, so each took a healthy swig from Dr. Branscomb's bottle, and in a short while Wilshire, Annabelle, and Rhoda, were all sound asleep on the floor of the swaying railway car.

Upon their late evening arrival in Christiansburg, Wilshire explained Rhoda's situation to a ticket agent who solicited a waiting freight wagoner to transport Rhoda and family to the Hospital. It was in the morning of the next day before Rhoda was finally examined by a resident. The doctor who finally saw her was an elderly gentleman who was well practiced at setting broken bones and performing amputations on injured soldiers and miners, but he was reluctant to perform abdominal surgery on Rhoda. Connecting what Wilshire told him about Rhoda's high fever to the disappearance of her pain, the doctor shared his opinion that her inflamed appendix had ruptured and it was likely that she was soon to die from peritonitis. He suggested that Rhoda's best chance would be for them to take her on the Norfolk and Western train to Roanoke where she could seek treatment at the new Lewis-Gale Hospital, one of the most modern facilities in the state. The doctor would be able to telephone Lewis-Gale to inform them of Rhoda's pending arrival and provide a summary diagnosis. If Rhoda was still alive when she arrived, there she might be saved.

The hour-long trip on the Norfolk and Western passenger train from Christiansburg to Roanoke was of a speed and comfort level beyond anything any of them had ever imagined. Thanks to the telephone call from the doctor in Christiansburg, a Model-T ambulance was waiting at the Roanoke train station, and from there Rhoda was rushed to the Lewis-Gale Hospital, given a hasty examination, and quickly taken into surgery.

The surgeon began the operation by making perpendicular incisions along the right side and across the upper part of Rhoda's abdomen, each of them several inches long. The objective was to create a large triangular flap in the abdominal muscles which would allow access for irrigating and sponging out the gangrenous pus from the peritonitis that the surgeon expected to find. But turning back the abdominal flap revealed no peritonitis and exposed a perfectly healthy appendix. Exploration into the upper abdomen, however, revealed gall stones and a badly infected gall bladder. The gall bladder and several large stones were removed, along with the unoffending appendix, and just two days later Rhoda appeared to be out of danger.

For the first couple of days they in Roanoke, hospital policy allowed Wilshire very little time with Rhoda, but that gave him the opportunity to ask around to figure out just where they were and how they could eventually get back home. Once it was clear that Rhoda was on her way to recovery, Wilshire began to make serious plans about first getting himself back. He could assume that the neighbors would be looking in on the children and that someone would take care of the cows and pigs, but he had left his horses in care of the smithy in Sylvatus, and he was unsure of what kind of care they were receiving. After getting someone who knew the route from Roanoke to Sylvatus to sketch him a map, Wilshire headed back toward Sylvatus, walking.

Wilshire was told that if he followed the road, the trip from Roanoke to Sylvatus would be about 50 miles, but he reckoned that he could walk the trip in three days. To someone who often plowed for fourteen hour days, this prospect did not seem especially formidable. As Wilshire approached the foot of Bent Mountain, however, he was able to hitch a ride with a teamster driving a freight wagon from Roanoke to Floyd, and that enabled him to make it to Sylvatus in just two long days. After boarding for a night in Sylvatus and retrieving his team and wagon, he returned to Laurel Fork.

Rhoda was in good hands in Roanoke, especially with Annabelle there to help look after her, and as soon as word got around that Rhoda was in the hospital, the neighbors in Laurel Fork inundated Wilshire and family with more food than they could possibly eat. Wilshire had been worrying and fretting at home for two more days before he was relieved by the first letter from Annabelle. She posted letters daily to keep Wilshire informed of Rhoda's progress, and three weeks from the morning they had first set out from home, Wilshire received a letter telling him of the plans for their return.

Annabelle had been advised that the easiest way to transport Rhoda from Roanoke to Laurel Fork would be for them to take the Southern Railways train from Roanoke to Danville. From Danville, they could take the Danville and Western train to Stuart, and there Wil could meet them with the wagon to carry them up the mountain and home to Laurel Fork. Rhody and Annabelle were going to leave Roanoke early on the morning of April 16, but they would arrive in Stuart so late in the evening that it would be best if Wilshire could arrange for them to spend the night there.

The Danville and Western Train, known as the Dick and Willie to the local wags, was little more luxurious than the Betty Baker train on which they had begun their journey. Requiring almost four hours to make the fifty mile trip through the Appalachian foothills from Danville to Stuart, the D&W was alleged to stop at most hen houses and all out houses in between. Laurel Fork was only twenty-five miles to the west of Stuart, but more than half of that distance was the climb up Lover's Leap Mountain, and the Danville/Wytheville Pike was always a muddy mess in April. On the evening of the 16th, Wilshire met his wife and daughter at the station in Stuart as scheduled, after having arranged for comfortable accommodations in the Perkins Hotel. Early the following morning they left on the last leg of Rhoda's odyssey, transporting her up the mountain from Stuart in the farm wagon.

As the wagon bounced and sloshed up the pike toward the top of Lovers Leap Mountain, Rhody sat half reclined on her pallet in the wagon bed, feeling almost euphoric as she drank in the green of the budding spring and retraced her recent travels in her mind. When she had left Laurel Fork on that cold morning, the trees had been bare. She had now been gone from her home for over three weeks, the longest period of time she had spent away from home in her life. She had traveled almost fifty miles from Laurel fork to Christiansburg, from there to Roanoke, and then from Roanoke to Danville. Every one of those places was farther from her home than she had ever been before. She had never even seen a train until this adventure, and now she had ridden on four of them. She had been bed-ridden for over two weeks, waited on hand and foot until she thought she could not abide it for another minute. She had been pronounced to be at death's door at least twice, but here she was, weak and sore to be sure, but very much alive! And now, in only three or four more hours, she would be returning to her beloved home in Laurel Fork.

Sloshing along the Danville/Wytheville Pike through Meadows of Dan, as they were riding by the lane that ran up to the house where Rhoda's sister Fanny lived, Rhoda had a sudden thought. "Turn in here," she told Wilshire, with such command in her voice that he did not consider questioning her instructions. Wil turned the team up the lane and pulled the wagon right up to the front porch of the house. He lowered the wagon tailgate, and with assistance from him and Annabelle, Rhoda slid out of the wagon and shakily stood. Then, while holding on to the side of the wagon, she reached back in and grasped the cane she had brought from the hospital.

"Wait here," she ordered, as she began hobbling slowly along the stepping stones, then grunting up and onto the front porch of the old white farm house. She was bent over from pain and exertion when she arrived at the door, so she paused for a long moment to regain her breath. Then she rapped sharply on the door with the handle of her cane.

Fanny opened wide the front door and gave a gasp of delight at the sight of her older sister. "Rhody, you're back!" she cried. "Tell me about everything that happened to you."

Rhoda took a deep breath, and for the first time in over three weeks, she thrust out her chin and straightened up to her full, magnificent six foot height.

"Well, let's go sit down, Fanny," she earnestly commenced. "I've been somewhere!"

The Salvation of Brother Emmitt

For most of Emmitt's adult life, folks had thought of him as a hard working farmer, a man who provided for his family the best that he could. But for the last couple of years, it had gotten so that every few weeks, Emmitt would go riding off up the pike somewhere and get his hands on a jug of corn likker. Once he got into that jug, Emmitt would keep nipping at it until every last drop was gone and he had become hopelessly and helplessly potted. It was fortunate for him that his faithful mare could find her way home without any help from Emmitt, but smart as that horse was, she could not open the barn lot gate. Usually, when they would arrive back home after he had been out on a toot, Emmitt would be so sotted that he could not even get down from his horse to open the gate. He would sit there astride his poor mare, hanging on to the saddle horn and hollering for his wife Jane or his daughter Barbara or his neighbor Solly, hollering for someone to please come help him down from his horse.

She had dealt with the situation so many times before that Jane suggested to Emmitt that maybe he could put a latch on the gate that he could open from horseback. Emmitt was highly offended by the suggestion, declaring that no latch would be needed, since he was never going to have another drink of likker for as long as he lived. Emmitt would usually declare that he was never going to have another drink at some point when he was in the painful process of sobering up from his most recent bender.

Every few weeks, there would be Emmitt, out at the barn lot once again, yelling for someone to come out and open the gate and help him down from his horse. If his good natured neighbor was at home and heard him hollering, Solly would stride across the meadow that separated their farms and help Emmitt clamber down from the saddle. But if the neighbor was unable to respond, Jane and Barbara would carry out bed quilts and pillows and arrange them in a pile beside the horse. Emmitt would then slowly lean over from the saddle until he fell from his horse, while Jane and Barbara tried to guide him onto the bedding as he fell. Emmitt was a rather tall and gangly fellow, and the unusual method of his dismounting would have been even more dangerous and difficult, had he not weighed less than a hundred and fifty pounds.

Then one morning, after Emmitt had been off on another of his excursions, Jane went out to milk the cow and found him lying unconscious by the gate. Jane had not expected Emmitt to be back so soon, and since it had rained through much of the night, she must not have heard him hollering over the noise of the rain hitting the tin roof.

Now there he was, lying in a puddle next to the barn lot gate, out cold and maybe even dead. Jane and Barbara dragged him into the house, pulled off his muddy boots and clothing and managed to get him up and onto the bed. Emmitt seemed to be breathing alright, but he was mumbling incoherently and was totally unresponsive to Jane's efforts to get him to tell her what had happened.

When Barbara ran to the neighbor's and told him what had happened to Emmitt, Solly insisted that he should go and get Dr. Branscomb right then. The doctor showed up at Jane and Emmitt's house about noon and began to assess Emmitt's injuries. It was obvious to the doctor that Emmitt had suffered a powerful blow to his left side of his head and that he had a broken collar bone. He may also have had other internal injuries, the doctor said, but he really couldn't tell about that just yet. Emmitt would occasionally flail about and jabber, and he seemed totally unaware that there was anyone else around.

When the doctor cleaned Emmitt's head injury, an angry contusion and pronounced swelling was revealed. The doctor had Jane hold a cold compress on the head injury and then later she held onto Emmitt's feet while the doctor pulled the collar bone into place and bound his upper arm tightly against his torso. Dr. Branscomb was unwilling to give any prognosis for a recovery, other than to say that the patient probably had a serious concussion and everything depended on how much his brain would swell through that day and the next. He left a bottle of clear liquid to be administered to Emmitt, but only if he became conscious and appeared to be in pain.

It didn't take long for word of Emmitt's misfortune to get spread around in Pike City. The preacher showed up about suppertime that night, and neighbors began dropping in, leaving dishes of food all through the next day. Sheriff Webb even showed up the next afternoon, partly to express his concern about Emmitt's condition, but also to inquire as to whether there had been any foul play.

Judging from Emmitt's injuries and his examination of the scene of the accident, the sheriff reached the conclusion that a very drunk Emmitt was leaning out from the saddle while attempting to unlatch the gate without dismounting, a maneuver that would not have been easy for someone who was stone cold sober. The sheriff guessed that Emmitt had fallen out of the saddle and hit his head on the gatepost on his way to the ground. His collarbone was probably broken when he hit the ground. "A fall like would have probably killed a sober feller," was the sheriff's profound conclusion.

The Reverend Thom Worley was a regular visitor at Emmitt's bedside for the days following the accident, both praying fervently for healing and talking quietly and earnestly to Emmitt, hoping to elicit some kind of a response. It was five days after the accident that Emmit first responded with a nod in response to a question the preacher asked him. The next morning, when Jane walked into the room, Emmitt opened his eyes and asked her what time it was and when did she think the preacher might be there. Emmitt's recovery was speedy from that point on.

A couple of months after the accident, when Reverend Worley stopped by to check on Emmitt one afternoon, he asked to talk to the preacher with no one else around. Jane's feelings were a little hurt by the request, but she left the room without protesting and closed the door behind her. While Jane didn't actually press her ear to the door or anything like that, she did stay close by, and she could not help but pick up a word of their conversation here and there. Emmitt seemed to be telling the preacher about how much remorse he felt over the kind of life he had been leading, and now that he had stared death in the face, he was determined to turn his life around.

The reverend responded by assuring Emmitt that he was now on the right track, but that it was very difficult for someone to change unless he was willing to turn his life over to the Lord. What Emmitt really needed to do, according to Reverend Worley, was to not dwell on the past, but to accept the forgiveness offered by grace and to concentrate on walking a different path from this day forward. It would surely help if he would start coming to church, the Reverend said, and he should sincerely ask the Lord to help him give up likker altogether. Then the reverend and Emmitt began to quietly pray together, but Jane could not make out any of that conversation.

A few minutes later, a beaming Reverend Worley came out of the room. "Brother Emmitt has just made the most important decision of his life," he informed an astonished Jane. "He wishes to be baptized in the spirit and become a member of the Cold Spring Church."

*****

The long walk up Oak Knob had required considerable effort for the Reverend Thom, but the view from up there was so gratifying that he quickly regained his strength, taking in the morning air in long, deep breaths of satisfaction.

Although the Reverend Thom Worley was a man of considerable girth, the struggle required for him to make the hike across the knob had as much to do with his state of anxiety as with the pull of gravity. For the entire walk up that hill, he had been imagining that he might look down from the summit toward the Cold Spring Church and see a silent and empty church yard.

But now he could see both a buggy and a surrey pulled up under a large maple, the horses tied to the tree trunk. A Model-A Ford Sedan, an old lumber truck, and a muddy Model-T roadster were parked in a line on the side of the dirt road in front of the little white church. Several horses were tied to trees near the church, and he could see Brother Steven tying his mule to the railing beside the front steps, just as he had done every Sunday for the past twenty years. He could even see a small group of men clustered outside of the church. They were probably reluctant to give up their chews and their smokes and move inside, the Reverend assumed.

Many members of the congregation walked to the services, so even the few conveyances he could see around the building indicated to the Reverend that the church would be nearly filled. The Good Reverend's anxiety then returned as he began to worry about just why so many had decided to come to the church that day. Had they come just because they all wished to weigh in on the controversy that the church would be dealing with that Sunday?

The Reverend had a lot of influence with the people in the community though. He had grown up in those mountains, and he understood the mountain culture and truly loved the people. When he had first been called to the Cold Spring Church, he had been able to reunite the squabbling factions that had nearly destroyed it. He promoted the rather liberal position that the individual is the master of his own salvation, and that salvation is granted through grace alone, not by works, and certainly not by some special incantations of the minister. He told the members of the church that they should prayerfully search within their own hearts to learn what beliefs they should hold on

62

troubling issues, and at the same time, they should maintain fellowship with the others in the church, even though they might believe somewhat differently. After all, did Jesus Christ not dine with Gentiles and sinners? They could discuss scriptural interpretations among themselves if they thought it would be helpful, but heated argument among members regarding the scripture would accomplish nothing. The result of the reverend's enlightened, moderate attitude was the establishment of a friendly truce among even the more doctrinaire members of the little church, in spite of some fundamental differences of belief.

Until just a week before, Reverend Worley had been feeling as though he was on the verge of uniting the church within a state of blessed concordance. But in a congregation like this one, a coalition of independent minded and sometimes ornery mountain people, discord is never far beneath the surface. Some of the theological differences had been brought to a head when Emmitt, once a respected community member but now a man cursed with an addiction to alcohol, had come forward at the invitation on a recent Sunday and expressed his desire to become a member of the church.

Emmitt, a blood relation of several stalwart members of the church, had come forward at the altar call on Sunday only two weeks before, confessing his transgressions and asking to be accepted into membership. A true reformation of Brother Emmitt would have been an event that would have enhanced the reputation the Cold Spring Church and the Reverend Thom as well, but at the moment Emmitt's salvation was to have been confirmed, he had backslid in a most egregious manner. The issue at hand was whether the baptism had been consummated sufficiently and Brother Emmitt had truly been saved, or if the entire process needed to be repeated from the beginning.

The Reverend had learned right much human psychology through his experience as a minister, although he didn't call it that. It could have been just good old common sense, but whatever the label, it had worked before and perhaps it would work again. To someone who did not know him, the Reverend Thom might give the impression of a gruff and rugged mountain man, someone whom you would take care to not provoke. But to those who knew him best, the members of his congregation, he was a compassionate minister and a master of gentle persuasion. The carefully crafted sermon Reverend Worley had given to an overflowing congregation in the Cold Spring Church that morning had been the easy part. Now, before the benediction could be pronounced, there was a delicate matter that had to be brought before the congregation. A decision had to be made, and it hinged on an interpretation of church doctrine. The more time he allowed to pass before facing the matter, thought the Good Reverend, the more likely it would be that the congregation would make an uncharitable decision.

The reverend called the church into session and the clerk immediately turned the proceedings back over to the Reverend, who introduced the matter at hand with humility and tact. "Even those of you who were not here on the afternoon of the Sunday past must surely have heard about the unfortunate disruption that arose at the baptismal service of our Brother Emmitt," he told the congregation. "Before we proceed, I would like to review the details of that service as well as I am able to recall them, and if I am judged to be in error, then I will stand to be corrected."

The reverend began by reminding the congregation of how they had all been praying for the salvation of a community member who, for so long, had been considered to be hopelessly lost. "It was just two weeks ago today that Brother Emmitt stood before this congregation and declared that he was renouncing his old way of living and was now determined to follow the path of righteousness," recalled the Reverend. "Oh, how his words of contrition filled all our hearts with joy. He confessed that he was lost, but that he was assured that he would be forgiven and redeemed by the power of grace. Brother Emmitt also stated that he wished to become a member of this church and to publicly confirm his salvation through the rite of baptism as soon as possible."

"Brother Emmit's baptism was scheduled for the very next Sunday afternoon, and like most of you, I believed that this baptism would be a most significant event in the life of our church here. What better thing can happen than sheep that was so dismally lost, now is found and brought into the fold."

The good reverend then called the congregation into session and began to describe the details of Brother Emmitt's baptism for the church record. He vividly described how he had been looking forward to Emmitt's baptism, and how distressed he had been to observe the condition of the candidate upon his arrival, for it had been obvious to everyone there that Brother Emmitt had thoroughly fortified himself for the impending baptism.

The Cold Spring Creek ran just a few yards behind the church, flowing between the glade below the church and along the edge of a large wooded area on the other side. For longer than anyone in the church could remember, there had been a wooden dam across the creek, built there to create a wide baptismal pond near the church. The pond, which by that time had been used for baptisms for more than half a century, was the center of a serene and idyllic setting, a quiet retreat that inspired a sense of peace and reverence in all who came there. There were willow and birch trees overhanging the pond on one side, and a level, grassy area right beside it on the other. Folks attending a baptism could park by the church and take the short walk down the slope to the glade beside the pond, where they could comfortably stand and watch. If a large crowd was in attendance, late arrivals could stand on the slope all of the way up to the church and still have a good view of the proceedings. People could even comfortably sit along the top of the slope and observe the ceremony if they so desired.

There could be a problem for some attending a baptism at the Cold Spring Church Baptismal Pond, however, because of the steep path that led from the church down to it. Walking down the path may not have been much of a problem for most folks, but it could be a challenge for the very young or the very old or for the highly inebriated.

On the Sunday morning before the baptism, the scheduled time of two o'clock for the ceremony had been announced in church. Now, as the time approached two-thirty, many of the folks who had gathered around the pond were beginning to wonder if Emmit was going to show up at all. A confident Reverend Worley was busily reassuring those who were considering giving up and going home, when Solly Alderman's Model-A Ford came chugging down the Cold Spring Road and stopped right at the top of the path leading down to the baptismal pond.

If folks were relieved to see Emmitt and Jane arriving in Solly's car, they were also dismayed to see that it took all the strength that Solly and Jane could muster to pull Emmitt from the car and to hold him upright. In fact, Reverend Worley and some others had to hurry up the hill to assist in delivering Emmitt down the path to the side of the Pond.

The Reverend Worley eloquently described the initiation of Emmitt's baptism to the congregation: "Upon beholding the sorry state of Brother Emmitt, I could only put my trust in the Lord that our brother could still receive the gift of salvation, believing with all my heart that a state of grace is sufficient to overcome a state of inebriation."

"How my heart filled with joy as we sang that old hymn, Shall We Gather at The River, and when I asked Brother Emmitt if he was prepared to accept Jesus Christ as his personal Lord and Savior, it sounded to me like he declared with great certainty that he was ready. I say 'sounded like,' because Brother Emmitt doesn't speak any too clearly when he is cold sober, and when he has been partaking, it is hard to understand a word he says."

"As the congregation sang and we proceeded into the baptismal pond, Brother Emmitt was having such great difficulty remaining upright that I latched onto his shoulder with one hand and grabbed onto his belt in the back with the other, as Brother Solly assisted from the other side. As I led him into the waters, I was thinking of how wonderful it was that this lost soul was about to be saved from the clutches of sin. But Old Satan, don't you see, he does not give up so easily. And on this day, beloved, Old Satan had well-laid plans."

Reverend Worley then described how, as they had waded into the pond until the water was about up to their knees, Brother Emmitt had suddenly stopped, pushed up against the preacher and began softly yammering into his ear and nodding over toward the willow trees. To those who were close enough to hear Emmitt, it sounded as though he said something like, "Nadda odder okatan ober dere?" It had sounded like a question to the Reverend, so he had assumed the candidate was seeking reassurance. The preacher sought to calm Emmitt's fears as they continued on into deeper water. It never occurred to anyone there that Brother Emmitt might have been trying to warn the preacher that there was a serpent lurking nearby.

As they reached a part of the pond where the water was about waist deep, Brother Emmitt began to resist again. "Nadda odder okatan ober dere?" he repeated more loudly, this time pointing into the canopy of trees overhanging the pond.

The preacher was not about to interrupt the baptism at this point. He began repeating the baptismal creed as he literally carried Brother Emmitt into chest deep water, and he struggled with him again as he turned him around in preparation for his submersion. At that point, the candidate for baptism became violently uncooperative, and all Preacher Worley could do was to hold on and give his shortest invocation ever. He described the termination of the proceedings as follows:

68

"I was in the process of submerging Brother Emmitt in the baptismal waters when a serpent descended from an overhanging limb and splashed into the pond right next to our brother, and just as Old Satan arrived in his best known incarnation, Brother Emmitt's speech became remarkably clear and distinct."

The good reverend did not quote Brother Emmitt verbatim to the congregation, but everyone who was at the baptism had heard exactly what he had said.

"Snake, snake, hit's a Goddamned snake!" Emmitt had screeched, as he wrenched free of the preacher's grasp and lunged for the bank!

The preacher sadly described the termination of the baptismal ceremony to the congregation. "Brother Emmitt had vanished in an instant, and I myself departed from the baptismal waters shortly thereafter, without even pausing for a benediction. I humbly acknowledge that Old Satan indeed carried that day. Now, Brother Emmitt refuses to even come to his door and talk with me, and I have not laid eyes him since. Brothers and Sisters, should any of you see our dear wayward brother, please assure him that he is forgiven. Confirm to him that his confession and baptism are sufficient for his salvation. Assure him that the Lord loves him still and considers him one of his own. Call upon him as one of our flock and tell him, should he return to the fold, he will be truly welcomed."

"Now, there is an issue at hand which, I believe, requires a vote by the congregation. I have searched the scriptures diligently during the past week, and I am assured that, in spite of the early conclusion of his baptism, Brother Emmitt's salvation is complete and eternal. The question that remains is whether Brother

Emmitt is officially a member in good standing with this congregation."

"While the scriptures do not tell us that a full immersion baptism is required for salvation, our Rules of Church Order do state that baptism by submersion is required for membership in our denomination. Now, it may be that Brother Emmitt was never completely submerged, for Beloved, you as well as I, saw our brother run all the way across the waters of the Cold Spring Baptismal Pond and out through the woods. We, Brothers and Sisters, were witnesses to a miracle."

"Therefore, do I hear a motion that we accept Brother Emmitt into the fellowship of the Cold Spring Church, with all of the rights and privileges granted to its members thereof?"

Long Before Amazon

It was not so very long ago that if there was something that someone needed to buy, they simply went to the local general store and bought it. If they didn't have the money or the general store didn't have what they needed, they just made do without it. The needs of the folks in Rural America used to be a lot more basic than they are today, but if someone thought they needed something a little out of the ordinary, there were always merchants who would be quick to tell the customer, "We don't have it right now, but we can get it for you in just a day or two." But now, good roads and Walmart have just about done in all of the general stores in America, and for those that haven't already been done in, the internet is poised to finish off.

Almost everyone I know orders stuff on line these days, and who can blame them? It is a convenient way to shop, it is quick and easy to compare prices, and in some cases, you can even avoid the local sales taxes.

Do-it-yourselfers can often locate hard to find items on line and avoid having to burn up a lot of time and gasoline by searching from store to store. Not long ago, I was able to go on line and order a minor part for our dishwasher and make the repair myself. Since that kept me from having to call a repairman, it obviously saved me some significant money. My wife was not happy about having to wait several days to get the dishwasher fixed, however, especially when she found out that I could have gotten the part delivered overnight for only an additional twenty dollars or so.

Over the past few decades, the major home improvement chains such as Lowes and Home Depot have been successful in driving almost all of the traditional neighborhood hardware stores out of business. Now that these same stores are complaining about how all of the internet shopping is hurting their own business, I am less than sympathetic. I still buy a lot from those home improvement stores, and while I may be able to find a better deal on light bulbs or vacuum cleaner bags by shopping on line, I don't expect to be ordering any two by fours or lawn fertilizer over the internet any time soon.

While we do hear a lot of concern that internet shopping, especially shopping through a giant like Amazon.com is going to be the end of the brick and mortar stores, I think such concerns are overblown. While the internet has hurt some businesses, it has helped some others, and this sort of thing has happened before, you know. Does anyone remember the lowly mail order catalog? Do you not remember Sears Roebuck & Company? Spiegel? Montgomery Ward?

While shopping has obviously been made more convenient by the internet, it is really just another form of mail order. Back in my parents' and grandparents' day, the great mail order houses like Sears Roebuck and Co. and Montgomery Ward were the sources of a large share of the worldly goods owned by many Americans. I'm guessing that those two companies alone were the source of more possessions and for a larger percentage of American homes than Amazon.com provides for them today.

Mom did not drive and Dad worked all of the time when I was a young child, with the effect that a majority of the everyday items used by my family were obtained through mail order. From the overalls and shoes that I wore to school, to the plates from which we ate our food and the pots in which it was cooked, all of these goods were conveniently delivered to our homes by the United States Postal Service just a week or two after Mom had mailed in the order to Sears Roebuck or Montgomery Ward. And although Santa Claus wasn't terribly generous to my siblings and me, the few things he did bring us looked an awful lot like stuff we had been drooling over as we looked through the Sears Christmas Book. The items we found in our Christmas stockings, including the socks and mittens, made it appear as though that Santa Claus did most of his shopping at Sears Roebuck, just like Mama did.

Of the incredible range of stuff that could be obtained through mail order, there were two live commodities that could be obtained through the mail that continue to amaze me whenever I think about it. One could purchase either honey bees or baby chicks by mail order from any of several different sources. They would promptly be delivered by the U.S. Postal Service as easily as it delivered wall paper or galoshes. I remember being at the Meadows of Dan Post Office one morning many years ago, when postmistress Gladys Reynolds pushed a buzzing wooden box with a screen wire front through the post office service window and onto the counter in front of a waiting customer.

"I'm supposed to be getting a queen and three thousand worker bees. Are they all in there?" the customer asked her.

"Well, do you want me to wait while you count 'em?" she responded.

There were a number of times, usually around March, when Levi West, our mail carrier, would stop on the shoulder of Highway 58 in front of house and blow his car horn. We had been expecting this to happen, and when I would run out to the carrier's car, he would hand me a flat cardboard box out through the car window, as though he was delivering a pizza. As I looked back into the car through the open window, I could see several similar boxes, all stacked up behind the carrier on the car's back seat.

The sides of the heavy duty cardboard boxes were perforated with a great many dime-sized holes through which one could hear and see great activity. A cacophony of peep, peep, peeps could be heard from the inside of the box, and occasionally, a tiny yellow beak would protrude through one of the holes. The box would bounce with life as I carried it back to the house. Some years we would receive two or three such boxes, each one containing one hundred baby chicks. Actually, the boxes usually contained a hundred, plus two or three more baby chicks, because there were always a couple that did not survive the shipping process. We almost always received very close to one-hundred <u>live</u> biddies per box, which is still pretty amazing, considering the several hundred miles those tiny creatures had travelled in the first two or three days of their lives.

Usually, we got our chicks from Sears, but there were many other sources from which live poultry such as baby chicks, goslings, turkey poults, etc. could be ordered. One year Dad responded to a radio advertisement that was broadcast over radio station WCKY, Cincinnati. The ad was for "Red Dot Baby Chicks," which were not only cheaper than those from Sears, but they were "one-hundred percent guaranteed

74

to *arrive alive and survive.*" Most of the chicks did just that, but because about eighty percent of the ones we received grew up to be roosters, we never ordered from them again. (Apparently, someone at Red Dot knew how to sort day-old biddies.) While we were waiting for those baby chicks to arrive, I remember wondering if we would we have to mail the dead biddies back to the company for our refund on any chicks that did not arrive alive.

Note: I had assumed that shipping bees and baby chicks through the mail was a thing of the past until just recently, when a friend from whom I buy eggs told me that he now orders his chickens through the internet. Upon checking on Google, I found an amazing variety of both chicks and bees available through the internet, delivered either by the U.S. Postal Service or overnight via UPS. I should have known, or I should have at least checked the internet. There is one big difference I should mention, however. I recall "Red Dot" charging us $9.99 for 100 baby chicks, including postage. The price for 100 baby chicks ordered via the internet todays is about $350.00, plus shipping. But live delivery is still guaranteed.

Since the very beginning of the mail order industry, the everyday term for the mail order catalog was the "wish book," and with good reason. On the rare occasion that someone had a little time to spare, they might relax by settling back in the chimney corner to peruse the Sears Roebuck mail order catalog and wish for some of those wonderful things it depicted. There were more than a thousand pages filled with pictures of marvelous merchandise, much of it luxury items that most folks in rural America could only wish for. It is true that much of what was available by mail order was of a utilitarian nature, things like saws and lanterns and washing machines, practical items that could be of great value to any farm family. But other, less practical and even more amazing items, were also displayed in those catalogs, things that many of the folks thumbing through the wish book may have never actually seen and could only dream about.

There were decorative items which surely would make any farm home more comfortable and livable, luxury items such as fancy clocks and dishes and upholstered furniture. There were pages filled with fashionable dresses and suits and shoes and hats, clothes so fancy that the folks examining those pages could not help but wonder where the people depicted might be going, all dressed up like that. The vision of urban America that existed in the minds of the denizens of the farther reaches of rural America must have been largely created by images seen on the pages of the mail order catalog. Probably, the nearest thing to pornography ever viewed by snickering little farm boys in the nineteen thirties and forties were the images of such gorgeous femininity as Lauren Bacall or Susan Heyward, as they modeled lingerie and corsets on the pages of the Sears, Roebuck & Co. catalog. (Those famous actresses really did model for Sears Roebuck, you know.)

One of the many wind-sucking preachers that could be heard on the local radio station when I was a kid spent a lot of time railing against the evils of mail order catalogs, declaring that they endangered the immortal souls of good people by tempting them to focus on worldly goods rather than their spiritual well-being, a temptation clearly warned against by the scriptures. Coincidentally, one of that preacher's sponsors was a locally brewed potion called *Dr. Hammod's New Medicine*, a bogus cure-all, available only through the mail from a post office box address. Sometime later, when the FDA finally investigated the "medicine," not only did they find that the concoction contained no useful ingredients, they found that it was being formulated in a galvanized washing tub under unsanitary conditions and that "Doctor" Hammod had obtained his medical degree by mail order.

As dependent as many Americans were on mail order in the years up to and during the Second World War, the popularity of mail order began declining just a few years afterwards. Soon after the war, developers began building shopping malls all over the nation, and a lot of those malls even had stores belonging to mail order companies such as Sears or Penny's. As the number of shopping malls increased, the distribution of the large mail order catalogs declined. Among the last mail order houses to discontinue the distribution of its large general catalog was Sears, ending its distribution of the big general catalog in 1993. The end of the Sears' big general catalog over twenty years ago did not mean the end of mail order catalogs, however. If most folks' experience is like mine, it is a rare mail delivery that does not include a few catalogs of one sort or another. Most of those slick publications I receive go directly from the mailbox to the recycling bin without ever being opened, but apparently not everyone is aware anything that they might consider ordering by mail can more easily be found and ordered on the internet.

Throughout her later years, my sainted mother, bless her heart, just loved to order stuff by mail. After she retired from teaching, Mom mostly liked to do two things. She liked to paint landscapes and she liked to look through the many catalogs she would receive in the mail. Of course, the more she ordered, the more catalogs that were sent to her. By now, most of us have figured out that anyone who actually orders from a mail order catalog gets their name placed on the universal sucker list. Mail order companies share their sucker lists with other mail order companies for a price, and if you order from any one mail order catalog, you are likely to become what is known as a targeted consumer. Somewhere in the cloud, a list of every item every mail order customer has ever bought has been collected, and that data is sold to other mail order companies, politicians, and special interest groups.

Once you buy from a mail order catalog, then the mail order harassment begins, or as was the case for my mom, the entertainment began. Many of the items she bought by mail order were not of very good value, but that was not the point. She just loved ordering stuff and then anticipating its eventual arrival, more or less efficiently delivered by the U.S. Mail. If the shopping channels had been available over broadcast television thirty years ago, Mom probably would have gone into bankruptcy.

At the very least, I can say this about Sears Roebuck and Montgomery Ward: When the things Mom ordered from those catalogs would finally arrive, they were usually pretty much as described. I think that much of the success of those two particular mail order houses was because they did offer decent quality for their prices, and they did honor the money-back guarantees they advertised. A lot of the stuff Mom bought from lesser-known mail order companies turned out to be junk, unfortunately, and good luck if she ever sent something back for a refund.

I sometimes wonder if Mom's romance with mail order had anything to do with the fact that her father was the mail carrier for Mayberry, Virginia, when she was a child. For his first twenty years as a mail carrier, he delivered the mail over a twenty mile route, riding either on horseback or in a buggy, depending on the weather and the quantity of mail. Anyone who remembers the size and weight of the Sears Roebuck or the Montgomery Ward general mail order catalogs can appreciate why Grandpa was not a big fan of mail order companies. He had to deliver about three hundred of those big catalogs two times a year, plus all of the smaller Christmas catalogs and sale books that were sent out in between. Fortunately, since a catalog was third class mail, he was not required to deliver them all on the same day. The delivery of those big general catalogs became less of an issue when he gave up his horse and buggy and began delivering the mail using a Model-A Ford.

How big were those old general mail order catalogs? Think of the Manhattan Telephone Directory. Until I was six years old, my booster seat for eating at the big table with the grownups was a big mail order catalog. By 1900, the Sears general catalog had grown to a size of about twelve hundred standard pages, and it remained about that large until near the end of the twentieth century. The catalogs were large enough that the Ward's and Sears' catalogs combined were sufficient to meet the annual outhouse needs for an average sized rural American family until indoor plumbing came along. There were a lot of unhappy customers back when the big mail order catalogs changed over from halftone images printed on cheap pulp newsprint to the high quality color photographs printed on slick varnished paper.

In addition to the size and number of the catalogs, a major problem the poor mail carrier of a century ago had to deal with was that folks could order almost anything from the big mail order companies and it would be shipped to them by the U.S. Mail.

My grandmother, the Mayberry mail carrier's wife was typical. She ordered just about everything you can think of; furniture, wall paper, a radio, a wood stove, and a chamber pot, all of them from Sears. She was a rather religious person and I think she may have believed that all of those good things being available via mail order was truly a wonder of the modern age, sent as a reward for the righteous people of the nation. Fortunately for Grandpa, he only had to transport the things Grandma ordered from the Post Office to their home. Unfortunately for him, other postal patrons also ordered large items, and all of those things had to be delivered out on the RFD mail route. Years after he retired, Grandpa could still reel off a long list of large items he recalled having had to deliver: washing tubs, dining tables (some assembly required), sewing machines, phonographs, horse collars, and garden cultivators, to name just a few. Anything that weighed a hundred pounds or less and occupied less than six cubic feet of space could be sent by parcel post in those days.

In the years prior to the Second World War, everything that was ordered from some distant mail order house was shipped by rail for most of the distance to the consumer. For example, most items ordered from

Sears, Roebuck and Co. were initially shipped out of Chicago by railway freight and the smaller items (less than 100 lbs.) were then forwarded from the railway depot to their destination almost exclusively by U.S. Mail. Really large items such as plows, anvils, or windmills, however (the Sears general catalog once listed several different models of each of those) were shipped from the manufacturer to the railway depot nearest the intended recipient. While there were fleets of horse drawn wagons and gasoline powered delivery vans for hire in large cities, it was up to the purchasers to arrange for the shipment of large items from the depot to their homes in rural communities such as Mayberry. In the early 1900's, most of the really large items shipped from Sears in Chicago and destined for someone in Mayberry, Virginia, were first delivered to the railway depot in a town about forty miles away that was known back then as *Pulaski City*, Virginia.

Eventually, large mail order houses established distribution warehouses in smaller cities, the Sears Warehouse in Greensboro, North Carolina, being one example. The proliferation of distribution warehouses certainly expedited the shipping of items, but it could mean that an order of several items might arrive piecemeal, an item which had been shipped from one warehouse might arrive at one time, and another item could arrive a week later because it was shipped from a different warehouse. For some folks, the arrival of their order being spread out over several days just made ordering by mail more fun.

Both of my grandfathers had farrier (horseshoeing) tools they had ordered from Sears. Grandpa Yeatts began shoeing horses when he was still in his teens, and sometime in the eighteen nineties he paid Sears Roebuck and Co. four dollars for a complete set of farrier's tools. The set included a *Manger's ABC Guide to Sensible Horseshoeing*, a book which Grandpa said he did not find to be all that helpful. He did find that his copy of *Howlett's Veterinary Practice at Home*, which he also ordered from Sears, was much more useful. That book became very important to him, since he treated his own livestock for all of their ailments. Over a period of several years, as he collected a few basic veterinary medicines and instruments (also from Sears), he became the unofficial animal doctor for much of Mayberry.

Although it is now possible to order just about anything on line from Amazon.com, some of us continue to associate that company with the sale of books. Well just for the record, the Sears Roebuck general catalog of a century ago also contained a very large book section. There were not many works of fiction to be found in the catalog, but there were many books on religion, philosophy, medicine, and manners. Sears specialty, however, was the how-to-do-it-yourself book. Sears carried a self-instruction book for just about any skill you could have thought of; sewing, gardening, blacksmithing, well drilling, brick laying, on and on.

Sometime around 1915, Grandma Yeatts decided that her family needed to start attending church on a regular basis. She wanted as many of the family as possible to attend together, and that created something of a problem. The nearest church was several miles distant, too far to comfortably walk even back when people walked almost everywhere they went. There were six kids in the family by then, and just four people could barely squeeze onto Grandpa's mail buggy. The farm wagon was the only other means available for transporting the family to church, and this was the same wagon that was used on a regular basis to haul firewood, hay, and manure. Grandma began insisting to Grandpa that the family needed a surrey (a buggy with two or more seats) so more of them could attend church together. She just happened to have found that the exact conveyance they needed was available for a reasonable price from the Sears Roebuck catalog.

Grandpa had been satisfied with the quality of the items that the family had bought from Sears in the past, so he finally agreed and took the plunge. He and Grandma ordered the family a surrey from Sears for the unbelievably low price of $74.90, not including the four dollar cost for shipping it from the factory in Kalamazoo, Michigan, to the railway depot in Pulaski City, Virginia. He also ordered a second set of harness and a doubletree, since the surrey would be set up as a two horse vehicle and his mail buggy was set up to be pulled by a single horse.

Several weeks after Grandpa sent in his order from Mayberry, he received a notice that the new surrey was ready to be picked up from the railway depot. Grandpa took a day off from carrying the mail and he and his oldest son, Coy, traveled to Pulaski City on horseback. Grandpa really did not expect that the surrey would arrive ready to hitch up and ride home, but he was surprised to find that it had been shipped flat in a crate and totally unassembled. Grandpa and Uncle Coy had to spend most of a day assembling the surrey before it could be ridden home to Mayberry. When Grandpa and Coy came home proudly driving the new surrey, not everyone was that enthusiastic. The older kids had convinced themselves that their dad was going to surprise them by driving home in a new automobile.

The Sears General Catalog of the early twentieth century listed a large number of heavy duty iron and steel products. Many of these tools for farm and industry such as anvils and wood saws were of the ACME brand, meaning they were manufactured by the ubiquitous ACME Steel Corporation of Chicago. One has to wonder if Wily E. Coyote also ordered some heavy duty iron products from Sears, Roebuck and Co.

My grandmother on my father's side never had much control over the finances of her household, but she managed to make some significant mail order purchases just the same. One fine day about 1930, she and grandpa put their heads together and decided that because they were now in their forties and getting on in years, they just ought to go ahead and get the inevitable over with. They agreed right then and there that the practical thing to do was for both of them to have all of their teeth pulled out and replaced with dentures. The very next morning, they hitched up the wagon and drove the six miles up Route 12 to the dentist's office at Laurel Fork. Both of them had every one of their teeth pulled that day, and then they rode their wagon back home that evening.

Grandpa returned to the dentist a few weeks later and was fitted for his new dentures. They were a little short of cash at the time, so Grandma decided to wait and see how well Grandpa's dentures worked out before deciding exactly what she was going to do about her own. While she was waiting, she came across an advertisement in the Planters' Almanac which claimed that false teeth could be purchased by mail order for as little as $5.00 per set, a price Grandma thought she could manage. The ad specified that a $1.00 refundable deposit to cover the cost of the denture impression kit should be sent in with the order coupon. The advertisement emphasized that anyone who was not completely satisfied with their new dentures could return them anytime within six months for a full refund, including the deposit. What did Grandma have to lose? She sent in her dollar deposit to Acme Dental Appliance Company (I am not kidding) and sure enough, in just a couple of weeks, the mail carrier delivered a package containing all of the materials necessary to make her own dental impressions, complete with detailed instructions.

The instructions that came with the impressions kit explained how to place the powder from the blue packet into the blue upper impression tray provided and then stir in just enough warm water to make a thick paste. The way that Grandma graphically described it, "I mixed up the paste in this little horseshoe-shaped box of a thing, and then I had to put that whole thing it in my mouth, bite down into it, and hold it there for at least five minutes. Lordy, that was the awfulest gaum!" A similar process using powder from the red packet and the red tray was required for the lower arch, and that was even more difficult and unpleasant. After making upper and lower impressions and allowing them to set up overnight, each was carefully packed into the special shipping box provided. Before everything was mailed back in, however, Grandma had to carefully fill out a form which included her checking the appropriate boxes to indicate the tint of whiteness desired for her new teeth and to select which of the three available colors she preferred for the gums.

Grandma followed the instructions meticulously and mailed in her impressions and the selection form, along with nine more dollars. (It turned out that the price was actually $5.00 each for the upper and for the lower dentures, but the cost of the impressions kit was deducted from that.) About a month later, she received her brand new teeth by parcel post. Grandma claimed to be perfectly satisfied with them, but I think they must not have been a very good fit because of the way they clicked when she was talking or eating. Her new teeth were unnaturally white and the gums were of a color similar to international orange, but Grandma never complained about them. They cost only a fourth of what Grandpa paid for his, and his did not fit all that well either. She eventually went to a dentist who relined her mail order dentures so that they would not click so much, and she wore them for many years.

Since her mail-order teeth were such a good deal, when Grandma realized that she needed some help with her vision, she followed up on an advertisement found in the same almanac. "Mail order eyeglasses, as low as $5.00. Satisfaction absolutely guaranteed!" She was required to send in a $2.00 non-refundable deposit this time, and a few weeks later she received her eyeglass fitting kit in the mail. The key component of the kit was a disk that had a series of small lenses arranged all of the way around the edge. A standard eye chart was included, along with a folding cardboard contraption that was supposed to help her determine the right size for the frames. The kit even included a twenty foot long paper tape measure, just to insure that she would read the eye chart from the correct distance.

The instructions explained how the disk should be held against the face so that it blocked the vision of the left eye while you looked at the chart through one of the lenses with the right eye. The disk was to be rotated and the chart viewed through one lens after another until the one that most improved the vision of that eye was determined. The number of the selected lens was to be recorded in the appropriate space on the accompanying form, and the procedure was then repeated for the left eye. The size and style of spectacles desired were also to be indicated on the form, as per instructions. There was also a card in the kit that had a diagram which illustrated how one could hold the card out in front and the arrows at the bottom would tell you which was left and which was right, if that happened to be a problem.

Grandma mailed in the form to the eye glass company, along with five more dollars, and sat back and waited. When Grandma received her new wire-rimmed spectacles just a few weeks later, the result was truly was amazing. They fit her face properly and corrected her vision perfectly, or so she claimed. The wire rims of the mail order glasses perfectly matched her severe countenance, and Grandma said that she considered her mail order spectacles to be every bit as satisfactory as her mail order dentures.

It is true that most of the items that were available by mail order could also be found in large department stores in cities across the country, but rarely at a competitive price. For years, the management of such stores complained bitterly about how the "unfair" competition from the mail order houses was going to be their ruin. But until the advent of the automobile and the construction of paved roads, there was really not much competition between department stores in the towns and the mail order houses used by the customers living out in areas of the country as remote as Mayberry, Virginia, or Oatmeal, Texas. There may have been a Globeman's in Galax, a Hieronymus in Danville, and a Belk's in Martinsville, but for someone who lived in Meadows of Dan, it took almost the whole day to go there and shop. Before the roads were paved, the weather could make the roads so bad that an overnight stay with a relative and a second day of travel might be required to complete the shopping trip. Considering the distance they would have had to have travelled and all of the difficulties involved, I think it is unlikely that either of my grandmothers ever set foot in one of those large city department stores. Thanks to mail order, however, they had access to most of the worldly goods they ever really wanted, both useful and frivolous.

Note: Some things come full circle. Recently I located the website for a company that sells eyeglasses on-line. The website allowed me to upload a selfie and try on all kinds of different eyeglass frames on my own face. With my ophthalmologist's prescription in hand, I was able to order my new glasses on line at a substantial savings. My mail-order glasses are completely satisfactory, but before you ask; no, I am not going to try buying dentures on-line.

One Man's Poison

Government projects that were created in response to the Great Depression made the thirties a time of prodigious road building throughout much of the country. One result of the construction and improvement of the highways was the appearance of a lot of new small businesses. As the roads across rural America were paved and the towns became better connected, tourist accommodations began springing up in response to the increase in long distance highway travel. Tourist facilities even began appearing along the 40 mile segment of U.S. Route 58, between Stuart and Hillsville, Virginia.

Until the bypass around Stuart was built, Highway 58 passed right through uptown. It approximately followed the route of what is now Blue Ridge Street, and if you think that is a crooked street now, you should have driven through town back in the day. In response to the increase in tourist traffic through the town, some entrepreneurial folks who lived beside Blue Ridge Street and had a spare bedroom or two put out signs, advertising their residences as "Tourist Homes." The nicer ones were kind of expensive, though, charging as much as four dollars per night. The Perkins Hotel down on Main Street had rooms for about the same price, but the hotel had been there for quite a few years and was beginning to show its age a bit. Also, the hotel was located a couple of blocks down Main Street away from the route of Highway 58 through the town, and in the absence of advertising, folks driving through the town might not have even known it was there.

For travelers who could not afford to stay in an expensive hotel or were uncomfortable spending the night in some stranger's home, the concept of the tourist cabin was created. The motor hotel, soon to become better known as the motel, had been introduced a few years earlier in California (Where else?), but in 1935 that concept was just emerging in many parts of the country. Along the stretch of U.S. 58 that connected Stuart and Hillsville, there were some interesting home-grown versions of tourist accommodations.

Smokey's Place, a few tourist cabins and a café, appeared in the late 30's. The establishment was squeezed in between the Mayo River and the highway, just to the west of Stuart. A few years before Smokey's, a small collection of very rustic tourist cabins had popped up on the side of Route 58 directly across from Robin Hood's Place, a little souvenir shop near the top of the mountain and right next to Lovers Leap. About twenty miles farther to the west and near Hillsville, the Silver Leaf Cabins were built behind an old general store that dated back to the days when the road was still part of the Danville/Wytheville Pike.

Tourist facilities such as Smokey's, places that had modern conveniences such as indoor plumbing and hot running water, did a pretty good business from the time they first opened. Even in the 1930's, most tourists were looking for accommodations with some minimum degree of comfort and convenience, but some of the new entrepreneurs were amazed to find that tourists expected such amenities. The hygienic accommodations a traveler might find in tourist cabins such as those at Robin Hood's Place would be a tin basin and a bucket of cold water in each of the cabins, with a single two-hole outhouse serving the calls of nature for all of them.

There were compensations available at some of the more rustic hostelries, however, to the extent that bootleg whisky could be provided upon request. And as hard as it may be for some folks to believe, I have even heard stories that indicated there were some of those "tourist" cabins along the way that may have been used for purposes other than the providing of a respite for weary travelers. There is a story I have heard that involved a couple of such places, and it just so happens that it also involved a favorite uncle of mine.

*****

Uncle Farley and his buddy Alfred really thought they had hit the jackpot at the Odd Fellows Dance that night. They had been furloughed from their jobs in West Virginia for a couple of weeks, and while using their laid-off time as an opportunity to spend a few days back home in Mayberry, they decided to go to the Saturday night dance at the Odd Fellows Hall. They had been making some real good money, at least by depression standards, and they had high hopes of running into some of the local girls they had known before they left the area. They were certain that they would be able to impress their former lady friends with their newly acquired affluence and sophistication.

Unfortunately, Farley and Alfred were unable to meet up with any of their old girl friends. It soon became clear to them that all of the single ladies of Mayberry that they used to know either gotten hitched or had moved on to greener pastures. The guys had not been at the dance for long, however, before they noticed a couple of girls on the other side of the hall who were kind of casting glances in their direction. Farley and Alfred quickly moved across the dance floor and sidled up to the two ladies to introduce themselves, even though up close, the "girls" turned out to be a little older than they had appeared from across the room. Uncle Farley, as usual, took the lead in approaching the two women, disarming them with his wise cracks such as "I saw the sign that said 'Odd Fellows,' and I figured that must mean us."

The women said they were from Hillsville, but Uncle Farley was kind of skeptical about that. He thought they sounded like they were from a ways off somewhere, but the important thing was they both seemed bubbly and fun-loving, and quite taken with the two young fellows. The gal that really took a shine to Alfred, though, kind of looked as though she may have danced a few dances too many. Both of the girls quickly indicated that they were looking for some fellows who knew how to have a good time, whatever that may have meant.

Farley and Alfred were not bad-looking fellows and they could be pretty charming when they made the effort. They were able to give those ladies the impression that they had enough money to entertain them in whatever way they would like. The Hillsville gals seemed to be especially impressed when they found that the guys had come to the dance equipped with hip flasks filled with some fairly decent hooch. At a time when the country was just coming out of the Great Depression and prohibition was still in force in Virginia, these spiffed up guys and their flasks made a big hit with their new acquaintances.

Any consumption or display of alcoholic beverages inside the Odd Fellows hall was strictly prohibited, but those in charge of the building had no control over whatever might take place in the parking lot outside. Farley and Alfred would enjoy a couple of dances with their new friends, and then they would all make a trip outside to take a quick nip from the flasks. This ritual had been repeated enough times that everyone in the group was feeling pretty happy, when the bootleg booze in the little flasks gave out. The four all agreed that it was too early for the party to come to an end, so they all put their heads together and came up with a plan to allow the festivities to continue.

Farley told the ladies that there was no problem at all, since he knew a place not too far away where they could get refills for the flasks. The girls left their car parked at the Odd Fellows Hall and they all piled into Farley's big old Hudson Terraplane, heading down Route 58 to Robin Hood's Place, only to find that the place was closed. Being closed down so early on a Saturday night could only have meant that Robin Hood's had also run out of booze. There was a backup plan, however, that only meant that the fun girls from Hillsville were treated to the half-hour trip down Lovers Leap Mountain from Robin Hood's to Sparky's. Alfred allowed that Robin Hood's Place being closed was actually a good thing, since they would be able to buy better booze at Sparky's anyway.

After the few minutes it took Farley to convince Sparky that he and Alfred were not A.T.F. agents, the group came into possession of a couple of pints of low-grade bonded hooch that had been imported all the way from Maryland. Thanks to the recent passage of the

21st amendment, the partiers were able to purchase genuine government bonded whisky from Sparky, but it was still some really rot-gut booze. While Sparky may have bootlegged a few bottles of bonded liquor into bone-dry Patrick County for his friends, he was certainly no moonshiner. He always limited his supply on the premises to sixteen pints or less, eight for him and eight for the misses, keeping him within the Virginia maximum legal residential possession limit of eight pints per person, just in case he ever got raided.

The party now had its supply of booze restored, but by the time they had driven back up the mountain to the Odd Fellows Hall, it was after eleven o'clock, the dance had ended, and everyone was leaving. When the girls said that they needed to get on back to Hillsville anyway, everyone agreed that if the festivities were to continue, they needed to move on up Route 58. Farley already had the Silver Leaf Cabins in his head as the logical destination, since they were heading in that direction. Farley and his new friend roared on up Highway 58 it his Hudson, with Alfred following along behind, chauffeuring his new friend in her Model A.

The details of the story as it was told to me became somewhat vague at this point, but apparently the partiers were able to rent both rooms of a duplex cabin at Silver Leaf, and the party continued until the small hours of the morning. Farley had brought his portable wind-up Victrola along in the Hudson, and long into the night, the partiers had played records and danced. They also continued to drink the hooch they had bought at Sparkey's, and the Lord knows what-in-all else may have happened there. Whatever it was, I was not told, but one thing Uncle Farley did tell me was that he suspended his drinking shortly after they left

Sparky's. He wanted to be sure he could navigate the road back up Lovers Leap Mountain, and he claimed that he didn't drink much more, even after the party had settled into the cabins. This was not his first rodeo, and according to Uncle Farley, whenever he drank, he was always careful to save himself a substantial snort for a kick start the next morning.

After the long night of partying, Farley awakened around noon the next day with a hangover that would be remembered for a long time. He soon noticed that his recently made acquaintances and their car were gone. Sometime in the night they must have moved on up the road, and that suited him just fine. Uncle Farley was in bad enough shape that he was sure that he would not be able to function at all until he had been medicated with a little "hair of the dog," but when he looked into the bottle that should have held his little eye opener, there was not a drop to be seen. After searching the room and finding only another empty bottle, he went next door and shook Alfred awake.

"Al, did you drink that last bit of booze I saved last night?" Farley was on the verge of panic. "What happened to the rest of my whisky?"

Alfred raised his head up from his pillow with a puzzled look on his face, unsure of what the commotion was all about.

Farley kept insisting, "Al, I know I didn't drink all of that booze last night. I know I saved myself a drink for this morning." Farley grabbed Alfred's shoulder and shook him. "Now do you know where the hell it is?"

Alfred sat up and scratched the cobwebs from his head. Finally, he began to recall what had happened. "Well, Far, I am afraid I used it up, Ol' Buddy."

"You mean you drank up the last bit of my booze?" Farley just couldn't believe his good buddy would do a thing like that.

"Well, I didn't drink it up," Alfred insisted. "I used it up. I used it for medical purposes."

"That's what I want it for, dammit!" snapped Farley. "I need it for medicine."

"Well, it's all gone now, but I didn't drink it," Alfred continued to insist. "You remember them ol' gals we were in here last night?"

Farley remembered.

"Well, I don't know how to tell you this, Ol' Buddy," Alfred wheedled, trying to soften up Farley. "But I woke up early this mornin' and I got thinking about that ol' gal I was with last night...and....," Alfred's story sort of faded out.

"What about that ol' gal?" Farley wanted to know. "Are you sayin' that she drank up my booze?"

"Naw, she didn't drink it. She was long gone when I woke up. What happened is that...well, I kind of got to worrying about my bein' with some ol' gal that I really didn't know. You know, she really did seem to have been around the block a few times. I really don't know how to tell you this, but...I kind of had a medical emergency." Alfred was having a real hard time letting the story come out.

Alfred paused, then blurted it all out as quickly as he could. "I got so dang worried, just thinkin' about what could happen that I got up and used up the rest of your likker. I poured it..."

"What do you mean you used it up? You poured it out?" Farley interrupted.

"You gotta' give me a chance to explain," Alfred insisted. "I didn't just pour it out. I poured it onto my pekker."

"You what?" squawked Farley.

"You know, to sterilize it," Alfred lamented. "I was thinkin' that maybe that likker might keep me from catchin' something serious. But I'm sorry about your booze, ol' buddy, really I am."

Farley just stood there in that dumpy little room, not really believing what he was hearing. Then, as he thought about what Alfred had done and why, the whole ridiculous business suddenly seemed hilarious. As Farley held onto his throbbing head, he doubled up while laughing through the pain.

"It's OK, buddy," he told Alfred as soon as he could breathe. "It's OK. I reckon I really would call that a real medical emergency. I just hope it works."

The Right Stuff

When I was first told that the two brothers, neighbors of ours, had both become fighter pilots for the United States Air Force, I was not at all surprised. Although they were a few years ahead of me in school, I could remember them well, since all twelve years of our public school educations were conducted in the same single building. Their family lived only a couple of miles away, and that made us neighbors by the rural Appalachian standards of the time. These were boys who, from their very early childhood, exhibited behavior that would indicate that flying jets was exactly the sort of thing they would love to do. Both of them were top students academically, they both played sports, they helped their dad run a dairy farm and a store, and they still found time to get into plenty of minor mischief. The boys' daring inclinations were especially evident when they were teenagers.

On many Friday or Saturday nights in the early fifties, we would hear the whine of the engine in their daddy's 1949 straight-eight Buick Dynaflow from about a mile away, as it accelerated up the straight section of Highway 58 toward the Parkway. Half a minute later, the car would moan over the crest of the hill, past the church and the store, and whoosh down the hill on another straight section of road that ran past our house. Dad thought they must be going about a hundred miles per hour at that point, given how the blast of air from the car that would shake the windows as they blew past.

"Those boys must be trying to kill themselves," was a typical comment from my dad, as the big green Buick whined by at a very high speed. But kill themselves they did not, even though it was reported that each of them had, on several occasions, driven that big Buick through the Tump Spangler Bend at speeds exceeding 70 mph. Some less intrepid drivers had been done in by that tricky curve while trying to negotiate it at speeds not much more than fifty, but neither one of the brothers ever wrecked a car. While my dad would periodically declare that the boys were lucky to still be alive, he would have to grudgingly admit that they must be able to drive pretty well. Although I was about five years too young to be getting my driver's license, Dad would sometimes use the occasion of their speeding by to caution me that if he ever learned that I was driving like that, it would be the last time I would ever get to drive a car of his.

One summer morning in 1956, I happened to be out in a field near the road when a pair of F-80 fighter jets blasted in over the eastern horizon, flying low above Highway 58, then executing barrel rolls as they screamed past. They both made vertical climbs over the western horizon and then peeled off into opposing inside loops. After they passed each other above the highway they both did wingovers to again converge over Highway 58, then they headed back east and came thundering past in line, executing snap rolls as they disappeared in the direction from which they had come. Everyone in the neighborhood had come running out to see what the racket was about, but most of us had no idea who was flying the planes or why. Some feared that we were under attack, even though the U.S. Air Force star insignia on the planes were obvious.

A community resident who lived just a ways up the road later admitted that his two nephews had been making training flights out of Langley Field, the U.S. Air Force Base near Virginia Beach. That base is only about a half an hour away for someone flying above Route 58 in a jet fighter. They had been planning on giving their uncle a demonstration of their recently acquired flying skills and had warned him in advance to be ready for some excitement one day soon, whenever the weather permitted. These two young men had each graduated from Virginia Military Institute and had received their respective commissions one and two years before. They had been able to arrange their Air Force duty so that they had gone through their flight training together.

As far back as elementary school, the teachers of those two boys had noted that they both were smart, determined, and focused. But they consistently exhibited a pattern of daring behavior that went all the way back even before they were in public school, back to when they were really little guys, just three and four years old.

The old farmhouse that Kanie and Eunice moved into in the 30's had actually been built in 1893 and it was oriented so that it faced the Danville-Wytheville Pike from a distance of a couple of hundred yards. The pike was replaced by U.S. Route 58 in 1932, however, and the new highway was routed behind the house and very close to it. Before Highway 58 was built, the kitchen window of the house had looked out onto a large meadow bordered by woodlands. The new highway had changed the view from the kitchen window to one of a grassy embankment less than thirty feet away that was topped by a paved highway. But even with the highway intruding so nearby, Mrs. Eunice, as she was called by most folks, could still enjoy looking out of her kitchen window at the peonies, sweet peas, and climbing roses that continued to grow in what was left of her old back yard.

As she looked out the open window into her back yard on that pleasant summer morning in 1938, a bit of activity up the highway and some distance away caught her eye. There was some movement near the top of the hill about a quarter of a mile to the west that looked like two light-colored dots bobbling back and forth near the center of the road. She decided there must be two very blonde and short little people coming her way, but they were dodging back and forth as they approached, and they were travelling much too fast to have been just walking. When the animated objects were temporarily lost from her view behind the embankment, she decided she had better to go out and climb up to the road for a better perspective.

A very pregnant Mrs. Eunice puffed up the bank to the level of the highway and was astounded to see two little blonde-headed boys come zooming down the road. When they were close enough for her to determine what and who they actually were, she ran out into the road to head them off.

"Stop! Stop boys, stop!" she shouted. You boys stop right now! Boys! Boys! Stop right now!"

There were two little guys heading toward her, flying down the hill on their tricycles, hunkered over their handlebars and pedaling furiously, as they weaved back and forth across the middle of the road. As they approached Mrs. Eunice, they showed no inclination of stopping, in spite of her commands, but she was able to catch onto the shirt of one of them as he attempted to pedal on past her. She then grabbed onto an arm and held to it tightly, bringing one boy to a stop. When the younger one was captured and held at a stop, the older boy turned back and joined them.

"What on earth do you boys think you are doing?" Mrs. Eunice demanded.

"We are going to Stuart to get some ice cream!" announced the four-year-old, standing up over his tricycle and proudly pulling a dime out of his pocket.

Two little kids riding their tricycles to the store to get ice cream might not seem quite so remarkable until more of the details are known. First of all, the distance to their declared destination, the town of Stuart, was about sixteen miles from where the boys were stopped. So far, the boys had only pedaled from their home to the point where their quest had been interrupted by Mrs. Eunice, a distance of about two miles. That was, however, two miles traveled by two little fellows pedaling tricycles over a surface of rough, recently applied, tar-and-gravel pavement on a road with no sidewalks or even a graveled shoulder.

Those two boys, one of them three years old and the other one four, had ridden their tricycles down the middle of the highway for a distance of two miles. If Mrs. Eunice had not been able to stop them, there's no telling how much farther they might have continued. They had somehow escaped from their home without their absence being detected and had ridden right past their father's store. They had also just ridden past another general store when they were finally stopped by Mrs. Eunice.

Why did the boys not stop and get their ice cream at one of those stores? The answer is simple: In 1938, there was no electric power in Meadows of Dan, Virginia. The location nearest to Meadows of Dan where ice cream was regularly available was in Stuart, Virginia, sixteen miles of crooked road down the mountain to the east. The boys knew exactly where to find Hudson's Drug store, the nearest store that sold ice cream, and they were determined to go there.

Once she had coaxed the boys into moving their tricycles safely out of the road, Mrs. Eunice's next concern was to inform the boys' family of their whereabouts. She was sure that the parents must be looking for their kids by now, but she had a difficult decision to make. She did not have a telephone in her house, but the store at the top of the hill did have one, and she knew that the boys' father had a telephone in his store. She could call from one store to the other, if she could just get the boys to go with her to the store nearby. The brothers, however, continued to insist that they were going to Stuart to get ice cream. They absolutely refused to cooperate when Mrs. Eunice tried to talk them into riding back up the hill to the store. Both stubbornly clung to their tricycles and refused to even dismount.

Mrs. Eunice grasped the handlebars of both of the tricycles and tried to pull them up the hill with the boys stubbornly sitting on them. They resisted any motion in the direction away from Stuart, even trying to pedal their tricycles backwards. Mrs. Eunice was quickly exhausted. As she stopped to catch her breath, Mrs. Eunice considered the alternative plan of forcefully carrying the younger brother to the store so she could make the call and hoping that the older boy would follow her, but she was not sure but that the older one might not leave his younger brother behind and strike out for Stuart on his own. She attempted to bribe them, offering to buy them candy if they would go with her to the store, but they were not tempted. Both insisted that nothing other than ice cream cones would satisfy their current cravings, and they needed to be big cones of chocolate ice cream, to be precise.

Mrs. Eunice was finally rescued from her dilemma by a neighbor who happened to drive by in his pickup. Frustrated at being unable to reason with the boys, she waved the pickup driver to a halt, explained the situation to him and emphasized the boys' unwillingness to cooperate. The neighbor simply responded by saying "I'll go get their daddy." He turned his pickup around in the road and headed up the highway for the father's store. In the meantime Mrs. Eunice was at least able to convince the boys to move their tricycles to the shade of a tree beside the road, so at least they could cool off and rest a bit.

No more than ten minutes later, a car driven by the boys' father came speeding down the road and slid to a quick stop. Mrs. Eunice and the boys could all see that the brothers were in big trouble by the look on the fathers face. With no resistance and hardly a word of objection, the boys were lifted onto the back seat of the car and their tricycles tossed into the trunk by their grim-faced father. The father commented to Mrs. Eunice that that he had been watching the boys ride their tricycles around in the lot next to his store just a short while before. "They could have made it to Stuart before dark at the rate they must have been traveling," he observed.

The boys sat passively on the back seat as their father climbed in and turned the car around, but Mrs. Eunice, observing the angry scowl on the father's face, suddenly felt sympathy for them.

"Now, don't be too tough on them," Mrs. Eunice called out to the father. "You know how little boys love ice cream."

"I'm not making any promises," the father growled and then paused. "This is what I get for giving those boys a dime," he mused, starting up his car and driving away."

The Fifty-Eight Desperado

One Saturday morning about 1950, as my dad was driving the family to Stuart, we found that the traffic had come to a stop just west of Lovers Leap. Dad, who knew the Patrick County roads really well, pulled over onto the shoulder of the road and eased along until he came to an old dirt road almost hidden by weeds. There, we turned off of Highway 58 onto what my dad called the "old road." As he carefully maneuvered the old Dodge around the back side of the mountain from Lovers Leap Wayside, he told us that this used to be State Route 12, and that this was what most of the road from Meadows of Dan to Stuart used to be like. The old road was rough, rocky, and narrow, with some really steep drop-offs along one side. As we rounded a sharp bend just before getting back to Highway 58, Dad slowed near a wide place in the road. As he pointed out of the driver's window he announced, "Right there is where that man who shot Trooper Thomas left him lying in the snow to die."

That sure got my attention, but when I pressed my dad for details, he could only give me a sketchy version of the tale. Sixty-five years later, after having read a lot of old Virginia and North Carolina newspapers, I have learned a lot more about the story.

*****

There were few other cars on the road that late December evening, as State Trooper L.E. Thomas began following the late-model Pontiac along Route 58 through Patrick Springs and toward Stuart. When the Trooper had pulled up close enough to the Pontiac to read the license plate, he could see that it was just loosely wired onto the bracket mounted on the rear bumper. A license tag wired onto an old pickup wouldn't have merited a second glance in Patrick County back then, but a loose, flapping plate on such a late model high-end automobile sure didn't seem right. As the Trooper had pulled up behind the car, he had noticed that it was being driven in a slightly erratic manner, the kind of driving his experience and training had taught him might mean that the driver was a novice, perhaps had been drinking, or was just nervous for some other reason.

Virginia State Trooper L.E. Thomas had been a State Trooper for twelve years, but he had been working in Patrick County for only the past two. It was assumed that the tall, likeable native of Clifton Forge, Virginia, had been assigned to Patrick County because of his experience in the demanding job of patrolling rugged mountain highways.

The trooper was then headed back to Stuart and looking forward to the end of his regular evening patrol after a long twelve-hour day. He was more than ready to sign off and go home on that blustery winter evening, but he decided that the car he was following, and especially its driver, required a closer look. When Trooper Thomas sounded the siren on his Ford patrol car, the driver of the Pontiac pulled off of the highway and stopped in front of a closed orchard stand near the Post Office. The slight young man who climbed out of the car seemed sober and was polite enough, but he could produce neither his driver's license nor the registration for the Pontiac. He nervously shivered as he gave an explanation about how he had just recently purchased the car, but had accidentally left his license and the temporary registration with the dealer. The officer thought the young man looked awfully scruffy and unkempt for someone driving such a fancy new car, and he was wearing really lightweight clothing for such cold winter weather. The man also claimed that he was on his way to visit family in Lynchburg, but if that was where he was really going, he was surely taking the long route to get there.

Mobile two-way radios that provided direct communications among police cars and stations were being used in only a few large American cities in 1938, and that technology was certainly not yet in use in Patrick County, Virginia. The patrol cars being used by the Virginia State Police were equipped with special radio receivers, however. Bulletins informing the officers about road conditions, accidents, and alerts for wanted suspects could be broadcast from regional highway patrol stations and relayed to the officers on patrol by local sheriff's offices and police stations. Highway Patrolmen could not send radio messages from their cars, however, and the relay broadcast station at the Sheriff's Office in Stuart was in operation only during the day.

There simply was no quick and easy way for a rural law officer to check drivers' license and registration documents while out on patrol in those days. Although it seems archaic and risky by today's standards, Trooper Thomas followed the officially established procedure for dealing with drivers not in possession of their license or vehicle registration at the time. The trooper instructed the driver of the Pontiac to proceed slowly along Highway 58 toward Stuart, the county seat, assuring the driver that he would be following closely behind.

Trooper Thomas told the young man that when they arrived in Stuart to turn left just past the court house and pull into one of the parking spaces at the Sheriff's Office. The court house was unmistakable, the officer told him, and he would be able to see the sign for the Sheriff's Office as soon as he made the left turn as instructed.

From the Patrick County Sheriff's Office, the trooper would be able to call Richmond and at least verify that someone with the name and address given by young man did have a license and confirm that the plate number matched the make of the car. If the trooper could not make some verification regarding either the driver's license or the vehicle registration for the Pontiac, the young man would spend the night as a guest of Patrick County.

As the two cars were driving toward Stuart, Trooper Thomas began mentally sorting through the wanted persons' bulletins that he had recently heard broadcast. A bulletin he had heard just the day before flashed into his mind. There was a lookout issued in several states for an outlawed fugitive from North Carolina, described as a 19 year-old man of slender build, blue eyes, and thick dark hair. The suspect, Roy Kelly, was a prison escapee from Anson County, North Carolina, and he was now also wanted as a suspect in the murder of the Alamance County Sheriff and a Burlington Police Officer just two days before. The officers were killed in a shootout with four men who were encountered in the process of burglarizing a Burlington service station. The bulletin had also stated that Roy Kelly was believed to have fled the scene of the crime in a Pontiac sedan with Georgia license plates. In the law enforcement jargon of the day, the wanted man was described as "an armed and dangerous desperado." The car in front of the trooper's patrol car at that time was a Pontiac sedan all right, but it had Virginia license plates, and although the man driving it generally fit the physical description of the North Carolina outlaw, so far he had been completely cooperative. He really didn't seem much like a "desperado" to the state trooper.

The young man drove the Pontiac slowly along Highway 58 and into the town of Stuart as instructed, with the trooper following closely behind. Both cars slowed as they approached the court house, but when the trooper flashed his lights and gave a hand signal for the driver to turn left and onto the street behind the Court House, the young man floored the Pontiac's accelerator and went speeding off. With the officer in pursuit, the two cars went tearing through the town of Stuart, bumper to bumper. It was after ten o'clock at night, and with the weather so cold and miserable, there was no other traffic on the road. That was fortunate, as the two cars went careening through the foothills west of Stuart as fast as they could be driven, their tires squalling through every curve and the patrol car's siren screaming like gangbusters.

During the first part of the chase westward on Highway 58, Trooper Thomas's 1937 Ford patrol car could not quite keep up with the heavier Pontiac, but all that changed when they started up Lover's Leap

Mountain. On that very curvy road, the trooper's superior driving skills allowed him to catch up with the fleeing suspect, and starting at about Greasy Bend and on up the mountain, the road was covered with snow. As they raced farther up the mountain, the depth of the snow increased to several inches, and there the troopers' experience in driving on icy mountain roads became even more of an advantage. As they approached Lover's Leap, the officer began bumping the rear of the suspect's car with the bumper of his patrol car in an attempt to force the Pontiac off of the road. As they drove through a deep cut just before reaching Lover's Leap Wayside, the officer was able to give the Pontiac a hard bump that caused it to spin around and slide backward into the ditch and up against the bank on the left side of the road.

Trooper Thomas's patrol car slid past the suspect's car as he stopped, but the trooper quickly backed up and stopped directly in front of the Pontiac, blocking it in against the bank. The officer then directed his spotlight onto the suspect and told him to get out of his car with his hands raised. The suspect raised his hands, but as the officer was climbing out of the patrol car, the suspect suddenly produced a gun and began shooting at the officer. Officer Thomas returned fire, and in the exchange, the Trooper was critically wounded in the chest and the suspect was possibly wounded in his hand. Officer Thomas collapsed unconscious into the snow.

In an analysis of the crime scene that was conducted later, investigators concluded that the suspect must have driven the patrol car a short distance with the unconscious state trooper inside. The suspect was believed to have driven the officer's car away from Lover's Leap and then turned off of Highway 58 and onto the roadway of old State Road 12, driving along the old roadbed only until he was out of sight of the main highway. The investigators speculated that the outlaw assumed that the unconscious trooper was dead and tried to move him into the trunk of the patrol car. At some point, the suspect apparently dropped the officer's car keys into the snow, and being unable to find them, abandoned the patrol car, leaving the unconscious Trooper lying in the snow beside it. The suspect then must have walked back to the Pontiac, where he was able to get the car out of the ditch and head back down Highway 58 toward Stuart.

After a length of time estimated to have been as much as an hour after the suspect had fled, Trooper Thomas miraculously regained consciousness. He later testified that when he came to, he was aware that he was bleeding from his mouth and chest, and he knew that if he could not get back into his car and drive for help, he would either freeze or bleed to death before anyone would find him. With all the strength he could muster, the trooper dragged himself back into his patrol car. Once inside the car, the officer discovered that the suspect had taken the keys from the car but that the ignition switch had been left in "unlocked off," which allowed the 1937 Ford to be started without a key. Officer Thomas was able to start the car and drive it around the back of Lovers Leap on the narrow old roadbed and back out onto Highway 58. He first drove about a half mile west to Lovers Leap Tavern, but it was now past 11:00 pm and the tavern was closed. The trooper then drove another mile westward, stopping at the first house he came to, the home of Henry Cassell and his family. Barely conscious when he stopped in front of the Cassells' house, the trooper activated the siren on his patrol car in a desperate attempt to get help. Henry Cassell came running out of his home and found the critically injured trooper bleeding out in his patrol car, now unable to speak. Recognizing that the trooper must be suffering from shock and the loss of blood, Mr. Cassell got a quilt from inside his house and wrapped the trooper in it. He then drove the injured officer to the Stuart Hospital in the patrol car. Mr. Cassell drove the unfamiliar car as fast as he could manage on the slippery road, and on the trip from the top of the mountain to Stuart, the Trooper again lapsed into unconsciousness.

While Dr. Walter Akers and the small staff at Stuart Hospital fought to save the Trooper's life, Mr. Cassell called Sheriff Frank Mays from the hospital to inform him that the State Trooper had been shot. Both the sheriff and the Commonwealth Attorney Frank Burton immediately came to the hospital to interview Mr. Cassell and begin the investigation, even though Officer Thomas could not yet be interviewed. As a precaution, Mr. Cassell was not allowed to leave until the investigators could obtain more information about what had happened to the injured officer.

Until Trooper Thomas regained consciousness the following day, there was little on which to begin the investigation. But Sheriff Mays had searched the patrol car the night before and found a note pad on which the trooper had written down the model and the license number of the suspect's car. In a marathon telephone call to Richmond later that night, commonwealth attorney Frank Burton was able to determine that the license plate had been stolen from an automobile in

Henrico County, Virginia, just the day before, information that was of little help at the time.

When the injured Trooper was able to talk a little, he told the sheriff that he was sure that the man who had shot him was Roy Kelly, the North Carolina escapee and outlaw. A day later, Trooper Thomas was able to confirm the identification from a photograph. The man who shot him was indeed Roy Kelly, and the trooper told Sheriff Mays that he may have also wounded Kelly in the exchange of gunfire.

After state-wide bulletins were issued for the fugitive, reported sightings began coming in from all over the state, first from Floyd, Virginia, then from Petersburg, and then Hopewell, but none of those could be confirmed. As the search for the fugitive Roy Kelly became more widespread and wanted posters were distributed nationally, sightings were reported as far away as Nebraska and Texas, but of course, none of those were confirmed either. Roy Kelly had grown up in rural North Carolina and had never lived in a large city, causing some experienced investigators to think that he had probably not fled to some very distant location.

About two weeks after the shooting of Trooper Thomas, the Virginia State Police received a call from a man who lived in a rural area north of Danville, Virginia. The man reported that someone fitting the description of Roy Kelly had recently sold him a .38 caliber revolver. A check of the serial number on the revolver showed it to be Trooper Thomas's officially issued side arm that was believed to have been taken by Roy Kelly after he shot the officer.

On Saturday afternoon, December 31, 1938, the Police Chief in South Hill, Virginia received a tip that

Roy Kelly was in a small restaurant located on the outskirts of the town. Police chief C.L. Templeton, two town constables, and a state trooper waited outside of the restaurant until Kelly emerged, where they surrounded him with their guns drawn. Roy Kelly was arrested without incident, although he claimed to be Clyde Harris from Statesville, North Carolina, for a while before admitting to his true identity. Kelly's right hand was heavily bandaged, and although he insisted that he had injured his hand while changing an automobile tire, an examination of the injury showed it to be a gunshot wound.

Roy Kelly told the police a series of wild tales about having been in Florida and Mississippi for the past three weeks, even claiming to have run police road blocks and engaged in shoot-outs with police on several occasions. The arresting officers, however, believe he had simply been laying low in the South Hill area of Southern Virginia for the whole time they had been looking for him. The Pontiac that Roy Kelly had been driving the night that he encountered Trooper Thomas was found parked behind the restaurant. There were bullet holes in the door and it was still bearing the stolen Virginia license plates that were wired on to the bracket and had attracted the trooper's attention in the first place.

The restaurant at which Roy Kelly was arrested was located right beside U.S. Highway 58, the same highway where, 140 miles farther west, he had shot the State Trooper three weeks before. A .45 caliber revolver was found under the driver's seat of the stolen Pontiac, and the back seat of the car was packed full of camping equipment. All of this gave further credibility to the theory that Roy Kelly had spent the weeks between the shooting of Trooper Thomas and his capture hiding out somewhere in the Piedmont Region of Virginia.

Kelly was held in the jail in South Boston, Virginia, while he was awaiting his transfer to the state penitentiary in Richmond, and during that time several newspaper reporters were allowed to interview him. This time, Roy Kelly entertained the reporters with fantastic tales about his brief life of crime, almost none of which could have possibly been true. In addition to the fabrications he told regarding his adventures as an outlaw on the run, he also claimed that the trooper attacked him as he was getting out of his car after it had been wrecked in the mountains. He claimed that as he and the trooper were fighting, the trooper drew his gun and was shot accidentally in a struggle over the weapon. Kelly also claimed to have put the trooper inside of his patrol car before he fled, asserting that he would never have abandoned an injured man and left him lying in the snow.

Upon learning of Roy Kelly's capture, the State of North Carolina immediately requested his extradition to stand trial for the murders of the Alamance County Sheriff and the Burlington Police officer. Patrick County Commonwealth Attorney Frank Burton wanted the State of Virginia to retain custody of Roy Kelly so he could be tried in Patrick County for the attempted murder of Trooper L. E. Thomas. Eventually however, after North Carolina officials signed an agreement to the effect that Kelly would be returned to Virginia to stand trial, should he be found not guilty, or neither sentenced to death nor to life without parole should he be convicted, the State of Virginia agreed to his extradition.

Roy Kelly was then extradited to North Carolina to stand trial for the murders of Alamance County Sheriff M.P. Robertson and Burlington Police Officer B.W. Vaughan. He was convicted on two counts of first degree murder in Burlington, North Carolina, and April 22, 1939, and sentenced to be executed in the gas chamber in Raleigh, North Carolina. The execution was first scheduled for a date of a little more than a year after he had attempted the murder of Virginia State Trooper L.E. Thomas, but the sentence was tied up in appeals for almost three years.

"Roy Kelly Dies in Raleigh Gas Chamber," was the headline printed in the Martinsville Bulletin on the morning of March 12, 1942. Although his execution was scheduled for 12:01 a.m. on that date, however, Roy Kelly did not die in the North Carolina gas chamber on that morning or at any later date. Hours before the scheduled execution, North Carolina Governor Clyde R. Hoey commuted Kelly's sentence to life imprisonment. Evidence was provided to the Governor that, although Roy Kelly had participated in the burglary in which the North Carolina Officers were killed, the deadly shots were fired by a participant who had himself been killed in the shootout, and that Kelly actually had been unarmed at the time. Roy Kelly's sentence was later commuted to 25 to 30 years of imprisonment, but then he was paroled in July of 1951 after serving only 12 years, a period of incarceration that included the time he had spent in prison while awaiting trial.

Upon learning that Kelly had been released, Virginia sought to extradite him to stand trial for the attempted murder of Virginia State Trooper L.E. Thomas. To the surprise of Patrick County officials, Roy Kelly voluntarily returned to Stuart to stand trial.

During that trial, Kelly repeated his claims that the trooper had been accidentally shot by his own gun while he and the trooper were fighting, and that he had moved the unconscious officer from the snow and into his patrol car before fleeing.

The physician who had treated the state trooper on the night he was shot and during the trooper's long battle for survival effectively refuted most of Kelly's claims. Dr. Walter Akers testified that the locations of the gunshot entry wound and the location of the projectile within the trooper's body, as revealed by x-ray images, indicated that the shot that wounded him had to have been fired from a direction almost perpendicular to the trooper's body. This would have been impossible if the trooper had been holding the gun. The doctor also testified that the x-ray images of the trooper's wound showed a projectile that was larger than .38 caliber, one that was probably a .45 caliber bullet.

Dr. Akers also told the court that when the wounded officer had been first brought to the hospital, his body temperature was been several degrees below normal. The doctor expressed his opinion was that the officer must have lain in the snow as much as an hour or more. Being in the snow for that length of time would have lowered the trooper's body temperature, which in turn slowed his heart rate and reduced the amount of bleeding. Ironically, having been left lying in the snow probably helped to save the officer's life.

In Stuart, Virginia, on June 19, 1952, Roy Kelly was found guilty of "felony aggravated assault while resisting arrest" and was given a sentence of seven years. Kelly's lawyers immediately appealed to Virginia Governor Battle for a parole, providing testimony that the defendant had been totally rehabilitated during the years he was in the North Carolina State Penitentiary and that he had been living as a model citizen during the time since his release. That appeal was unsuccessful.

WHOL

When the county agricultural extension agent first began talking about how background music in the dairy barn might result in an increased milk production, my dad thought it was a joke.

My own reaction was to ask the obvious questions: "Any particular music? Do cows respond differently to Grand Opera than they do to The Grand Ole Opry? Do cows like rock and roll?" Mr. Olinger, the county agent, said he didn't know about that, but he did go into some more detail about how the music in the barn theory came about.

Mr. Olinger, who was a very knowledgeable individual, even told us about some research that was done way back in the nineteen twenties. There was this study on *workplace efficiency,* as he called it, conducted at The Hawthorne Works, a Western Electric assembly plant located near Chicago. He said that the study showed that even minor changes in the work environment, changes in the intensity of the lighting, the height of the work surface, and of course, the presence of background music, could have a positive effect on worker productivity.

Agricultural researchers at places like Virginia Tech took notice and began conducting studies on how the environment in which dairy cattle were milked could affect milk production. Some factors such as the level of lighting and temperature seemed to have little effect, but they did conclude that the presence of background

121

music in a dairy barn could result in a slight increase in milk production. Naturally, I tried to convince my dad that putting a radio in the barn would be worth a try.

The extension agent must have really spread the word. Before long, everyone we knew who milked a few cows had a radio playing in their barn during milking time, and that included us. But when we first took the radio down to the barn, it did not have much of an effect on anything. The barn was kind of down in a hollow and it had a metal roof, so we could hardly get any radio reception in there at all. We could barely even pick up a radio station that was just a few miles from us. But then one morning in 1949, a station with the call letters WHOL-AM began coming in loud and clear. We heard the station manager announce that the station had just increased its broadcast power to 2000 watts. Soon, the announcers began to refer to Station WHOL as "The 2000 Watt Voice of the Blue Ridge Mountains!" Folks kind of laughed at that bit of hubris, since almost everybody knew that clear channel stations such as WCKY in Cincinnati and WBT in Charlotte broadcast at 50,000 watts at night.

On the other hand, two thousand watts seemed pretty powerful compared to what we had been trying to listen to before. What we did know for sure was where there had been only pitifully weak radio signals and the music and static came and went with the weather, there was now at least one strong and reliable radio signal coming in strong and clear, every single morning. As that radio station trumpeted the fact that its broadcast wattage had been increased to 2000 watts, it became the default source of background noise for our milking. During our early morning milking time, radio station WHOL was there to provide us with just what we

122

needed; the news, the weather, and a little inspiration from the gospel.

We would know that we were running on schedule if the National Anthem was playing when we turned the radio on in the barn. Promptly at five thirty-five a.m., the Star Spangled Banner would end and the "world-wide" headline news would begin. The brief world news report was followed by the local news and weather, the beginning of which was heralded by the robust crowing of a rooster. The rooster crowing morphed into an advertising ditty that I can remember to this day. It went, "He's a life-long rooster-booster, for Casco's Egg Producer!" In other words, the morning news and weather report was being brought to us by chicken feed. I suppose that the crowing rooster was intended to be a wakeup call for the station's listeners, but most everyone where we lived had been up and about for an hour by the time the Casco Rooster had finished crowing.

Station WHOL, with its announcers touting its "whol-lotta news, whol-lotta weather, and a whol-lotta music" format, became standard early morning fare for us and for many of our neighbors. Unfortunately, the station's whol-lotta news, weather, and music promotion failed to warn listeners of the biggest whol-lotta of them all, a whol-lotta really dumb commercials. To be fair, the station did provide its listeners with pretty good news and weather coverage, and the morning programming included some segments featuring what was then called "hillbilly" music. That was the kind of music most folks in the WHOL listening area would have been tuned into anyway, if they could get it on their radios.

Unfortunately, the early morning musical fare on Station WHOL alternated with some truly awful hillbilly preachers. They were all sincere purveyors of the gospel I am sure, but some of them were just itinerant wind-suckers who would shout out their fundamentalist message for the first half of their allotted quarter-hour, and then beg for contributions for the remainder. (Contributions other than cash were apparently acceptable, since one of the preachers would sometimes remind the listeners that his car needed new tires and he would frequently mention his fondness for home canned tomatoes and peaches.)

Those who prevailed through that first fifteen minute sermon/begathon, however, were rewarded with a forty-five minute program of popular country music called the *Getup and Go Show*. Although the program was punctuated by a lot of really awful commercials, most of them home-produced by the station, it was tolerable because of the humor of the lively and personable announcer who conducted it every weekday morning. This country Music DJ promoted himself as Uncle Charley, the Dan River Fiddler, and on the radio he took on the persona of a cantankerous old curmudgeon. He would come on the air with patter such as "Mornin' farm friends, Ol' Uncle Charley's gonna be fiddlin' around here for the next little bit, bringin' you some music that will make your day a little brighter and your heart a little lighter." He sounded like somebody you would like to know.

Folks who had actually met him as he was putting in personal appearances promoting the grocery stores and car dealers that were his sponsors said that Uncle Charley was really an amiable person. He was actually a rather young man, they said, and he really was an accomplished fiddle player. Dad and I both thought he was a hoot, but not everyone appreciated him as much as we did. He tended to poke fun at everybody and everything, especially lawyers and politicians. Sometimes he even mimicked the preachers who preceded him, and we even heard that he almost got fired for casting doubt on the honesty of the salesmen at a car dealership that sponsored his show.

We usually got to enjoy some part of the Getup and Go Show as we finished the milking and cleaning up the barn, but before we got to that we would always have to endure a sermon. There was one preacher who was so irritating that even the promise of Uncle Charley coming on soon would sometimes not keep us listening. This particular self-styled man of the cloth claimed that his name was Daniel Dickerson, and he called himself "Reverend Dan, the Milk-Cooler Man." Right after the radio announcer would introduce "The Milk-Cooler Man," he would always end his introduction with the catchy slogan of "anytime, day or night." On the mornings that Reverend Dickerson was the radio preacher, if one of us passed by the radio, we would often switch him off. Dad said that he was worried that all of the hollering from the preacher's sermons might actually cause the cows to withhold their milk.

Now a radio personality, especially a preacher, who would give himself a title such as "The Milk-Cooler Man" may seem a little strange, but you have to consider the time and place. First of all, most rural ministers had day jobs back then, and I guess it was helpful for any mountain preacher to give the impression that he was truly a man of the people. And in those days, there were few modern devices as important to dairy farmers as their milk coolers. When milk coolers first came into use, they were basically just refrigerated tanks, and some of the first ones that were installed for folks in our area just weren't all that reliable. There were often a lot of milk cooler problems in the hot summer months when there were lots of lightning storms. If a cooler containing two days of milk production stopped working during hot weather, it could cost a farmer a lot of money. That would explain the significance of the "any time, day or night" slogan for a preacher who called himself "the milk cooler man." Of course, anyone who could repair milk coolers could repair home refrigerators and other electrical equipment as well, so the reverend didn't just work on milk coolers. But as the name Daniel Dickerson became better known to folks in the area, I would occasionally hear my dad and his friends making winking inferences that the "anytime, day or night" slogan might have another meaning.

We had been listening to at least a part of Reverend Dan's sermons following the news and weather on station WHOL two mornings every week for what must have been at least a year. These sermons were mostly focused on the standard radio preacher fare of sinfulness, damnation, and redemption, but his sermons would often include detailed descriptions of the many instances of woeful depravity and wantonness the good reverend had observed in his business travels throughout the area. These sermons would often end with dire predictions of the pestilences the Lord was going to visit upon those within the sound of his voice out there in radio land if they did not change their wicked ways, and he meant change them soon. "We are living in the last days!" he would ominously warn his listeners, sometimes ending his sermon with the option,

"You can change your way of living today, or you can bust hell wide open tomorrow!"

The many sins the Good Reverend described as having personally observed in process included the usual drinking, dancing, card playing, and so on, and they were often described at such length and in such detail that some folks began to wonder just where the preacher's milk cooler repairs had been taking him. But in many of his sermons, the Reverend Dan seemed to have a special concern about the sins of the flesh – harlotry, fornication, and so on – which, according to his firsthand observations, were approaching epidemic proportions out there in radio land. I'll have to admit that the Reverend Dickerson expanded my vocabulary of terms associated with sinful behavior considerably during the year or so that he was on the air, and eventually his sermons got so interesting to me that when Dad would suggest that I turn the radio off, I would try to find an excuse to keep it on.

But then came the Tuesday morning that it was no longer the milk-cooler man who was broadcasting the morning homily live from station WHOL. A new and much less animated preacher, a smooth talking stranger of whom we had never heard, was substituting for the Reverend Dan. There was a substitute again for the reverend again on Thursday, and when the next Tuesday came around and there was still no Milk Cooler Man, I'll have to admit that I felt a little disappointed. I had gotten kind of interested in hearing some more about this harlotry and wantonness business.

There was no official announcement from WHOL, but rumors began to circulate in the community that the milk-cooler man might not be returning to the air. Although I found the rumors truly hard to believe, stories were spreading that the Reverend might have harbored a bit of weakness of his own for those sins of the flesh he was so fond of railing against. Then I overheard some of the snickering adults gossiping at the general store. Apparently, the Reverend's reputation as a ladies' man was so well known that his "any time, day or night," motto was deemed to be particularly appropriate, and the whole sordid story eventually became known: The good reverend, a man of the cloth who had a wife and family, had run off with a well-to-do divorcee from town. The Reverend and the woman were last seen as they were driving out of town together in the woman's Buick convertible, allegedly headed for Florida or Myrtle Beach or some similar location known for its concentration of wantonness. The entire WHOL listening area was in a state of turmoil.

For some time before the climactic event (no pun intended), Uncle Charley had been slipping in little comments about the preacher when his own show followed the Reverend Dan's. One could have guessed that he was not a great fan of the Good Reverend, and now Uncle Charley had an opportunity which was not to be denied.

Not long after the Reverend's disappearance, Uncle Charley began dedicating some of the popular records he played on his show to the Milk-Cooler Man. One of the most frequent dedications he made to the Reverend Dickerson was *Don't Rob Another Man's Castle*, as sung by Ernest Tubb, the Texas Troubadour. And then came the morning when Uncle Charley announced that he was going to dedicate his entire country music program that morning to "The Reverend Daniel Dickerson, wherever he may be." Not only did he play the old favorite by Ernest Tubb, but he followed

128

that one with Floyd Tillman's *Slippin' Around,* and then he played Jimmy Wakely's *One Has My Name, the Other Has My Heart.* He played several more, all dedicated to The Reverend Daniel Dickerson (wherever he may be), and finally ended with everybody's long-time favorite, Eddie Arnold's recording of *I Want to Play House with You.* It was that very morning, as I recall, when it first occurred to me about how much of country music was focused on just one particular topic.

Wherever The Reverend Dan Dickerson may have been that morning, he must not have been as far away as Uncle Charley had assumed. No sooner had Eddy Arnold finished playing house and Uncle Charley had begun reading a commercial, when he interrupted himself with a strange observation. "Well, looks like we have a guest here in the studio today," Uncle Charley announced to his listeners. "Howdy Reverend Dan. Where <u>have</u> you been so long?"

Listeners could only hear one side of the conversation, but it seemed to deteriorate rather rapidly. From our end, the broadcast sounded something like, "Whoa there, Reverend, you can't come back here, we're on the air you know. Now back off Reverend, you just need to leave the studio. Now, we were just having a little joke here Preacher, no offense intended. You ain't supposed to be in here no way, Preacher!"

This conversation was followed by what might have been the sounds of a scuffle, possibly the crash of a chair being turned over, then we heard a few loud thumps and grunts... and then the microphone was silent. For several minutes, nothing could be heard from Station WHOL but a loud hum. Finally, the broadcast resumed when the station manager came on the air and profusely apologized for an interruption of the normal broadcast schedule due to "technical difficulties." For the remainder of the week, the station manager assumed Uncle Charley's role, functioning as the not very entertaining DJ on the Get Up and Go show.

By the next week, though, Uncle Charley was back on the air, continuing with his radio show as though nothing out of the ordinary had happened. But, although I listened very carefully, I don't think he ever mentioned the Milk-Cooler Man again. The police report in the local paper the next week did mention that a Daniel G. Dickerson had been charged with assault, but the name of a plaintiff was not given.

Some folks who saw Uncle Charley glad-handing customers at the local Plymouth Dealership on the following Saturday afternoon reported that Uncle Charley looked like maybe somebody had given him a pretty good thumping. When somebody asked him what had happened, he just laughed and told them he had been run over by a milk cooler. Hard to imagine how that could have happened.

The Only Way to Farm

The last full day of farm work I ever did was early in June of 1959. The son of a neighbor had graduated from high school on a Friday evening, and immediately after the ceremony, had asserted his newly earned independence by cutting out for the beach. The father, unaware of his son's plans, found himself in a predicament, with several acres of newly cut alfalfa on the ground and a weather forecast for rain. I agreed to help him out; that was what neighbors did back then.

That Saturday the two of us raked, bailed, and stacked about a thousand square bales of dense alfalfa hay, stashing the last bales in the barn loft late in the evening, just before the rain arrived. The next morning, my arms and neck were all covered with hives, and on Monday, when I went to the doctor, he told me that I was having a serious allergic reaction to something. When I told him that the hives had popped up right after I had been working in alfalfa, the doctor said the alfalfa was a likely source of the problem and that contact with alfalfa produces an allergic reaction in a lot of people.

Well, that was it for me – I was definitely allergic to farm work. Even though I have done hardly a lick of farm work in over fifty years, I do continue to maintain an interest in farming, but strictly as an observer. Now that I am mostly retired and can spend more time back here in these mountains, I take the time to watch farming being done whenever I have the opportunity. I finally feel that I no longer have to take the quickest route when I have to run an errand. If there is no immediate need, I can take the time to drive over some of the back roads, often traveling past farms and homes that once belonged to people of my parent's and grandparent's generation. Some of the folks who lived there and worked those farms two and three generations ago were my friends and schoolmates. There are some newer homes, here and there along the way, and still a few functioning farms, but I also see a lot of vacant houses and collapsing farm buildings.

It is interesting to note that the number of old milk houses still standing is now much greater than the number of old barns, probably because the wooden barns were built first and the cinderblock milk houses were added a few years later. Most of the hard-working mountain people who built the barns and worked these farms are gone now, and much of the farmland on which they worked so hard to earn their living is returning to woodland and scrub. The most common kind of farming being done in the mountains these days appears to be the pasturing of beef cattle, along with growing enough hay and corn to maintain those cattle through the winter.

The earliest recollections I have of anything related to farming go back to the years of the Second World War, a time when almost everyone I knew still worked their farms using horses. Some, like the widow who lived on a farm next to ours, tried to maintain a small farm even though she did not have the resources to keep a draft animal. Folks like her could always find a neighbor who owned horses and would plow their gardens and help harvest their hay for a modest fee.

Early one summer morning when I was about seven years old, I rode a couple of miles up Highway 58 with my dad as he went to help his Uncle Joel Williams get up hay. When we met up with my great uncle, he was driving his team of Percheron horses, pulling a load of hay from the field to the barn. When my dad lifted me up onto the wagon seat beside my great uncle, my uncle asked if I wanted to drive the team. Uncle Joel clucked at the horses to start them moving and then handed the reins over to me, telling me to hold them firmly but loosely and to not pull back. At first I thought I had been given a great responsibility, but I soon realized that the horses knew exactly where they were supposed to go, having already traveled the route several times that morning. But holding onto those reins and feeling as though I had control over those huge animals was one of the most profound feelings of importance I have ever experienced.

From what I have learned about the history of Appalachian farming, it appears that the farming methods still being used at the time of the Second World War had changed little over the course of the preceding century. For all that time, almost every rural family had a vegetable garden, a few milk cows, a few pigs, a flock of chickens, and they also had to maintain a cow pasture and a hay meadow. Most of them had a field or two in which they rotated the growing of feed crops such as corn, oats, and buckwheat. Most of the farmers cultivated their crops with the assistance of one or two horses or a mule. If a time traveling American farmer from before the Civil War had visited an Appalachian farm of the nineteen forties, other than the widespread presence of woven wire fences and the car or pickup parked in the yard, he surely would have encountered very few things that surprised him.

In the years just after the war, we would more and more frequently pass by farms and see the owners proudly tilling their fields using their new Case and Farmall tractors. Most of the first tractors we saw were in use "below the mountain," where the land was less hilly than on the mountain where we lived. Some years later, I was to learn that the mechanized farming methods that had dominated agriculture in the Midwest for the first part of the twentieth century had taken almost another half a century to find their way into many parts of the Appalachian Mountains.

My limited knowledge of farming methods experienced a major expansion in the summer of 1946. Because my dad had been away in military service, all of our crop fields and most of our pastureland had been leased out to someone who had planted them in oats the previous spring. Our home had literally been surrounded by amber waves of grain for several weeks before the morning when a team of horses pulled an odd clattering contraption into the oat field nearest to our house. The machine quivered and rattled as it was pulled around the field, the upright stalks of oats disappearing before it and reappearing as bundles dropped onto the ground behind it. That was a reaper, I was told, and as I could see, its function was to cut the stalks of grain and tie them into bundles.

Not long after daylight the following morning, I was awakened as a deafening parade of machinery came bumping and clanging down U.S. Route 58. I ran out onto the porch in time to see an enormous gray Case tractor with red wheels pulling a wheeled metal box the size of a small barn into the field near our house. I was told that the big metal box was Homer Harris's threshing machine, and that the contraption in line behind it, the one being pulled along by a smoking Fordson tractor of similar vintage, was a bailer. Two flat-bed wagons, each pulled by a team of horses, completed the parade. Later, while the men were busy placing the machines exactly where they wanted them, chocking the wheels and getting all ready, my mom walked me over to a farm wagon that was sitting nearby. I climbed up and into it as Mom was telling me that my job would be to keep the workmen supplied with water. I was to keep the water bucket filled and whenever a workman walked up to the wagon, I was to hand him a dipper full of water. She also handed me a clean dish towel, with the instructions that I was to use that towel to keep the bucket covered when no one was drinking. There was going to be an awful lot of dust in the air around there in just a short while, she explained.

The only time I was to get down off of that wagon, I was seriously told, would be to return to the house to get more water or for personal reasons. That was fine with me, intimidated as I was of all those big machines, and their loud commotion, but I hadn't really heard anything yet. I felt reasonably safe up in the wagon though, and it provided a great vantage point from which I could observe all of the activity. After much shouting, waving, and repositioning of the thresher and the bailer, the men seemed to finally have placed the machines just where they wanted them, with the threshing machine and the hay bailer parked side by side and in opposite directions. The big metal box that the Case tractor had pulled into the field soon sprouted a big pipe from one end and another one was across the top and down one side. When a wide chute was lowered from the other end of the big box, it really

135

didn't look so much like a barn anymore. The big old case tractor was connected to one end of the thresher with a wide leather belt and the little Fordson, facing in the opposite direction from the Case, was connected with a similar belt to the bailer.

The man on the big tractor pulled on a lever that started the belt moving and then the threshing machine began making an awful racket and a lot of dust. A man on a wagon with a pitchfork started throwing the bundles of oats from the wagon onto the chute and a clanking wooden conveyor carried them inside the big box. After just a minute, a stream of loose oat straw came blowing out of the big stove pipe at the other end of the thresher, and pretty soon it had spewed a big pile of straw onto the ground between the thresher and the bailer.

Later, the hay bailer was also put into operation, doubling the noise level. A man at the pile of straw near the end of the thresher started forking the straw into the top of the bailer, where this thing on top that looked kind of like a donkey's head moved up and down and stuffed the straw inside. Pretty soon, I could see a block of straw coming out of the bailer, moving down this long square chute that stuck out of one end. As the straw moved down the chute in short jerks, two guys were busy poking wires through the sides of the chute. When the straw finally got to the end of the chute, a bale of straw would fall out, all tied up with two strands of wire.

A little later, I watched as a man slipped a tow sack over the end of the big metal pipe that came down the side of the threshing machine. When he pulled a lever near the end of the pipe, the sack got all bulged up like a balloon, and when he removed it, I could then see that the sack had been filled up with grain. After a while, I could tell that everyone had a job and they all were working together to change those bundles of oats into bales of straw and sacks of grain.

All of these strange mechanical devices made a tremendous impression on me. Even as a child who had no inkling of how they actually worked, I could see that an enormous amount of time and human labor was being saved by those machines. When I told my dad about how impressed I was with the machinery, Dad laughed and said most of that machinery they were using was older than he was.

In the summer of 1947, on a trip out west to visit relatives in Colorado and Iowa, I had an opportunity to observe a completely different level of mechanized farming. As we rode through Iowa and Kansas, we would see enormous wheat fields in which there were groups of four or five huge red or green machines moving around the field in concert, a fifty foot swath of wheat disappearing before them and windrows of straw left on the ground behind them The machines were called combines, I was told, because they both reaped and threshed the wheat. As a group of combines would move smoothly around the field, a truck would periodically pull up beside of one of the combines and a big metal pipe would swing out from the combine and out over the bed of the truck, filling the truck with grain in a matter of minutes, but the trek around the field was never slowed. The neatly windrowed wheat straw left on the ground behind was being picked up by bailers that followed the combines around the field, leaving bales of straw behind. "This is the way farming is done in the West," my dad announced, adding that such methods would never work on the steep land of the Appalachian Mountains.

In the late forties and early fifties, however, tractors began appearing on most of the farms in the Blue Ridge Mountains. A few of them were the large Case or John Deere tricycle type of tractors, machines that appeared to be more suited for farming on the Great Plains than in the Blue Ridge Mountains. Some farmers opted for the new Farmall A or little Farmall Cub tractors made by International Harvester. The tractor most responsible for the mechanization of the small mountain farm at that time, however, was the Ford 8N. This small and simple tractor came out in 1948 (that's what the 8 in 8N stands for) with an initial price of about a thousand dollars. The 8N had a lower center of gravity than the competing row cropping type of tractors, an important feature for mountain farming. Ford tractors also had the Ferguson hydraulic three-point hitch, an innovation which made it much easier to connect and disconnect implements and allowed a tractor with an implement attached to turn around in a small space. In just a few years, the hillside farms of the Blue Ridge Mountains were literally buzzing with Ford 8N tractors.

Although most mountain farmers were now using tractors, many found that some of their farmland could actually be more difficult to work using a tractor than it had been using horses. There were fields that had been productively cultivated using horse drawn equipment but that were just too steep to be safely worked with a tractor. Also, even in the mountains, there is a surprising amount of land that is just too wet and boggy to be worked effectively using a tractor.

My granddad used to have a meadow beside Mayberry Church Road where I remember watching the hay being mowed by a sickle mower that was pulled by a team of horses and then raked into windrows with a horse-drawn dump rake. That soggy meadow would produce six to eight large stacks of hay each summer. Around 1950, my granddad turned the farming over to a grandson who had a new Ford 8N tractor. The first time that tractor was driven into the soggy meadow to mow the hay, it sank up to its rear axle in the soft bottomland. Today, that former meadow is mostly woodland.

Obviously, the revolution in mountain farming methods did not occur all at once. Many who bought new tractors could not afford to buy all of the additional new equipment they needed all at once. During the forties and fifties, there was a lot of "hybrid" farm equipment was being used in these mountains. It was hybrid in the sense that tractors were being used to pull equipment that was originally designed to be powered by horses. For years, it was not at all unusual to see a Ford tractor being driven across a hay field while pulling a sickle mower or a hay rake that was originally designed as horse drawn equipment. In addition to the person driving the tractor, the formerly horse-drawn mower or hay rake also required someone to ride and operate it, and the two-operator requirement reduced the efficiency of mechanized farming considerably. It was so hard for some people to make the transition from the horse to the tractor that there was a company in Utah that made a tractor that could be controlled from the seat of a dump rake or a sickle mower using reins, just like driving a horse.

In the years following World War II, a surprising amount of mountain farming was done with the help of the ubiquitous Army Jeep. Many GIs came out of service having had direct experience with the jeep and having been impressed with the Jeep's toughness, reliability, and the pulling capability of its four wheel drive. Some thought that this was a vehicle that could be used both for daily transportation and for farming operations!   Willis, the original manufacturer of the Jeep, even began making them available with hydraulic lifts and power take-offs, installed as options for use with farm equipment. The Jeep was perfectly adept for pulling an old hay rake or a spike toothed harrow, equipment that was originally designed to be animal powered. When farmers attempted to use a Jeep for plowing or pulling a hay bailer, however, even the four-wheel-drive traction of the Jeep proved to be insufficient.   The old military-style jeep was soon relegated to functioning as reliable road transportation in bad weather and becoming a popular vehicle for use by rural mail carriers.

About 1949, a new store, quite large by Blue Ridge Mountain standards, was built in Meadows of Dan. Along with just about anything else anyone could possibly need, the new store began selling Ford Tractors and New Holland farm implements. And oh-my-goodness, how those Ford tractors did sell. It was not too long after the new Ford Tractor dealership at the Agee and Banks Store had opened that Homer Harris, owner of the threshing machine described earlier, parked his big old steel-wheeled Case Tractor in the Ford Dealer's used tractor lot and drove off on a new Ford 8N.

Homer's big old Case tractor sat on that Ford Tractor lot for a long time, and its second summer there, it became the center of a heated argument among a group of young teenage boys. One boy ventured the opinion that someone should buy that big old Case, since it was obviously so much more powerful than any of those little ol' Ford tractors parked all around it. The son of the tractor dealer took great umbrage at that assertion and declared any one of the little rubber-tired Fords sitting on that lot could out pull the big old Case.

There was only one way to find out: In what I like to think of as an impromptu scientific experiment, the boys organized a tractor-pull, hitching up a new Ford and the old Case, drawbar to drawbar, in the middle of the tractor lot. The guy who declared the Case tractor to be the most powerful climbed onto its driver's seat, while the dealer's son was positioned to drive the brand-new Ford 8N. A third party agreed to serve as the official starter.

When the starter gave the signal, the two tractor drivers revved their engines, dropped their clutches, and let the machines rip! The little Ford actually did win the day, pulling the big old Case backwards across the tractor lot. It is likely that the Ford prevailed, however, not because it had a more powerful engine, but because the old-style cleated steel wheels of the Case could not gain traction on the graveled lot as well as the rubber tires on the Ford. The tires made the difference, but the win for the Ford came at a cost. The rear wheels of both tractors spun vigorously during the pull, throwing rocks and gravel against each other and all over the other tractors in the lot, dinging the paint on new Ford tractors and covering them with dust. The dealer's son may have been in trouble with his Dad, but it truly was a grand experiment. All of us who were there that day left with the realization that there is more to pulling a heavy load than horsepower.

Much of the mechanization of farming that occurred in the fifties was connected to the Post-Second World War boom in dairying. Many rural families that had kept a milk cow or two before the war expanded their number of milk cows to five or six or maybe even twenty when milk prices went way up afterwards. The government made it easy for farmers to get low interest loans, and all over the county, new barns and milk houses were built and herds of forty or fifty milkers became commonplace. All those cattle required feed, and that in turn required bigger tractors and harvesting equipment. Unfortunately, the investment made in new equipment and buildings failed to pay off for many.

Changes in government regulations regarding the handling of milk put many of the small operators out of business. Soon farms could sell only Grade-A milk, and Grade-A regulations required that a milking barn must have concrete floors and electric milking machines. The milk had to be stored in a cooler in a separate building until it was picked up by a tanker truck. There were to be no more milk cans sitting on the side of the road, waiting to be picked up by the open stake-bed milk truck.

Some farmers went out of the milk business while others borrowed money to upgrade their diaries to Department of Agriculture Grade-A Dairy Requirements. Many who upgraded were soon in difficulty, partly because the government continued to tweak regulations and subsidies to help the big mid-western dairymen at the expense of the smaller eastern dairy farmers. One after another, over the last fifty years, dairy farmers in southwestern Virginia have either switched to raising beef cattle or to truck farming or they have quit farming altogether. Patrick County, Virginia, for example, a county that had over one hundred dairy farms in 1950, now has only one. That one dairy has a milking herd of over 700 cows, and that number makes it a small milk factory by today's standards. I recently read about a dairy farm in Indiana that has a milking herd of 30,000 head and I also read that Russia is building a 100,000 cow dairy farm as an act of revenge against the European Union because of the economic sanctions Europe has imposed on them. Now milk is being used as an international economic weapon?

Although mechanized methods have totally taken over farming even in the Blue Ridge Mountains, most of the equipment used there is mostly of a smaller scale than that used in the large-scale farming operations that dominate agriculture today. My first personal observation of corporate farming using "monster" tractors occurred in the early seventies.

I was driving east along US Route 58, near Emporia, Virginia, when I passed through an area that I remembered as previously being mostly covered with pine trees. Now, several square miles of the sandy land had been cleared and leveled, creating several huge open fields. While driving along a straight stretch of highway that ran past a long open field, I caught up with an enormous John Deere Tractor cruising across the field almost as fast as I was driving along the open highway. The tractor had same-sized dual wheels, front and back, and I estimated the tires to be to be about eight feet in diameter. The tractor had an enclosed cab, obviously air conditioned, since all of the windows in the cab were closed on that hot summer day. The guy operating the tractor was apparently unaware (or did not care) that anyone was watching as he pulled an enormous five-gang disk harrow across the field at highway speed. He had a big smile on his face, a Mountain Dew in one hand, and a pretty young woman sitting on his lap. "Now that," I said to myself, "is the only way to farm."

At the time I was told that the expanse of level farm land had only recently been leased and cleared by some large foreign agricultural corporation. Years later, however, when I drove along that same stretch of highway, I found that those big fields had all either returned to piney woods or been filled in with comfortable suburban homes.

CHINQUAPINS!

There are but few souls around who can still remember the widespread extinction of *Castanea Dentata*, the American Chestnut, but there are many more who are aware that there was an extinction of the American Chestnut that occurred in the first part of the twentieth century. On the other hand, there seems to be hardly anyone who is aware of the fate of the American Chestnuts' humble cousin, *Castanea Pumila*, the Allegany Chinquapin.

The blight that extinguished the American Chestnut was first detected on a tree at the Bronx Zoo in New York City in 1904, and it spread so rapidly and proved to be so deadly that there was hardly a healthy producing chestnut tree remaining in Southwestern Virginia by 1930. Although the great chestnut orchards of the Appalachian Mountains were all dead by the time I was old enough to know about them, many people can still recall the grey trunks of the dead trees they would see standing in clusters on the hillsides when they were children. Although the living tree could not resist the blight, chestnut wood is very rot resistant, and the trunks of dead trees would sometimes stand like monuments in the old chestnut orchards for decades after the last tree had died.

The hardy little chinquapin bushes, however, continued to thrive in the southeast, especially in the Appalachian Mountains, through the 1980's. But now the chinquapin has been found to be vulnerable to the same fungus that killed off the American Chestnut, and there are just a very few surviving chinquapin bushes in the Blue Ridge Mountains these days.

The demise of the chestnut was both a frightening occurrence and an economic disaster for many people of the Blue Ridge Mountains. Most folks had little understanding of how the chestnut blight could occur, and when it arrived in Southwestern Virginia in the 1920's, it was almost as a precursor to the Great Depression. With those two great disasters arriving one after the other, it is no wonder that a lot of people became convinced that the end of time must surely be at hand.

As a small child, when I would sometimes accompany my family on walks in the woods, we would occasionally come across living chestnut sprouts springing up from the stump of a dead chestnut tree. "They will die soon," my dad would say, and sadly shake his head as he predicted the fate of those sprouts. Unfortunately, he would always be right. On rare occasions we would even find an American chestnut sapling with some burrs on the ground around it, and on even rarer occasions, we might find a few burrs with edible nuts still inside them. We were able to find and eat just enough that I have some recollection of how they tasted. I especially recall how much sweeter and more flavorful those chestnuts were in comparison to the nuts from the Asian chestnut trees that were planted to replace them. On those same woodland forays, we would often find healthy chinquapin bushes growing at the edge of the woods in great abundance.

Even in the last few years, I have continued to come across struggling chestnut sprouts on rare occasions, but I always find that the sprouts have died when I go back to check on them a year or two later. In the summer, I sometimes tramp through the woods on the land where my grandfather's chestnut orchard used to stand, specifically looking for chestnut sprouts. On the rare occasion that I do find one, all I can do is take a sound leaf back to the house and announce to anyone present, "Now this is what the leaf of the American chestnut tree looks like." My wife, who is a potter, can then make a clay objet d'art in the shape of the leaf of an American chestnut as a sort of a memorial.

While most people have more knowledge of the American chestnut than they have about the chinquapin, both the chestnut and the chinquapin are widespread natives to most of the eastern United States. More of a shrub than a tree, the dwarf chestnut or Allegany chinquapin, was once prolific east of the Mississippi, from Virginia to Florida. The chinquapin nuts are also much smaller than chestnuts, but they are quite edible, and both once served as an important food source for wildlife and humans alike.

In 1612, Captain John Smith became the first European to make a written description of the chinquapin bush and its nuts. Today, however, most people have not even heard of them. This is probably because the chinquapin grows on a bush instead of a tree, and being such a small nut, the chinquapin never had much significant economic value.

Where I grew up, in the Blue Ridge Mountains of southwestern Virginia, almost every deciduous forest had chinquapin bushes growing around its edge. Chinquapins were prone to grow up through rail fences, and if a field was left fallow for a few years, one of the first scrub plants that would overtake the land would be chinquapin bushes. I think it is a reasonable analogy to say that the chinquapin was to the American chestnut what the scrub oak is to the mighty red oak.

Back when chinquapins were plentiful, folks who ate those little acorn-sized nuts would begin eating them by biting through the leathery hull and cleaving the nut in half, then prying out the nutmeat with their incisors. Skilled chinquapin eaters could pop chinquapins into their mouths, bite them in two longitudinally, manipulate the halves around, pry the nutmeat out, and spit out the hulls without having used their hands for anything other than putting the nuts into their mouths. As in any natural food, worms were often found in chinquapins, but that was not considered anything to be worried about. A chinquapin worm bitten in two by someone eating the nut has never ever eaten anything but chinquapins itself. At least that's what we used to tell ourselves while we were eating chinquapins, worms and all.

Of more concern is the sharp little tuft of the burr that is often found clinging to the blossom end of the nut, burrs that can sure irritate the tongue of someone who is eating a lot of chinquapins. Here in the Appalachian Mountains, the much anticipated September bounty of chinquapins was often accompanied by the ripening of the Concord grape, both of which grew in abundance in the area. In the Septembers of my childhood, after we kids had abraded our tongues raw by opening and eating chinquapins and then sucked a lot of acidic Concord grapes out of their husks, it was not uncommon for us to get blisters on our tongues from over indulging in those two wonderful, natural treats. They were well worth the blisters.

It should be noted that before chinquapins are available for eating, they first have to be removed from the spiny burr that surrounds them. As the nuts begin to ripen, the burrs will begin to open on their own while they are still on the bush, and the wider open the burr, the riper the nut. When the chinquapin burrs first begin to open, the nuts have to be carefully pried from the inside of the prickly burr, and one's success in picking chinquapins has a lot to do with one's determination and tolerance for pain. But when the nut is fully ripe, it is so loosely attached to the burr that the slightest touch can cause the nut to fall free and be lost on the ground. Chinquapin picking has never been for sissies or for the impatient.

In the mountains of Southwest Virginia three or four generations ago, a good chinquapin crop could represent a real economic windfall from a kid's point of view. The general stores in the area would usually buy chinquapins from the folks who had picked them, but the store would then ship them off to somewhere else to be sold, as no local individual would be willing to be seen buying chinquapins. The price paid by the local stores was not very much, with twenty-five cents per pound being the highest price I can remember being offered. It should be noted that a whole pound of chinquapins is really a lot of those little nuts, and it really represented a lot of sore, burr-stuck fingers. But there was a better deal than just 25¢ per pound to be had, especially for the kids who lived "out on the road," near a major highway such as Route 58 or the Blue Ridge Parkway.

The best deal we could get from selling chinquapins was to sell them to the tourists who were traveling on the Blue Ridge Parkway. Usually there would be two or three of us who would work together on a Sunday afternoon, often locating at an intersection such as the Parkway overpass at Highway 58 in Meadows of Dan, or the intersection of the Parkway and Rt. 8 at Tuggles Gap. We would fill a glass tumbler with the nuts, then stand on the shoulder of the Parkway, holding out the tumbler while yelling "CHINKEY PINS!" at the tops of our lungs whenever a car was approaching. Selling chinquapins was mostly a boy's job back then, probably because of the yelling requirement.

Once in a while, some tourists would stop, usually just to satisfy their curiosity about why we were yelling or to see whatever it was that we were trying to sell. Sometimes we would have to first convince the interested parties that the little nuts were not actually acorns and that they really were good to eat. Often we would have to demonstrate by eating a few ourselves, first to prove that they were edible, and then to demonstrate how to eat them. When a tourist would buy a tumbler full of the nuts, the nuts would be poured from the tumbler into a little number two paper bag before being presented to the buyer. This was not like buying Tuberose snuff – the tumblers did not come with the chinquapins. The nuts were initially placed in glass tumblers just to provide visibility. The tumblers (jelly jars, usually) that we used held about a quarter of a pound of the nuts and we often sold them for 15¢ to 25¢, much more than the price per pound we would get from selling them to the general store. I think I may have made six or eight dollars selling chinquapins on a few bright September Sundays, and that was a lot of money for a ten year old kid, in terms of 1950's currency.

Of course, the Blue Ridge Parkway Rangers would chase us off the Parkway whenever they caught us selling chinquapins there. Back then it sometimes appeared that the Rangers thought the Parkway was exclusively for the enjoyment of tourists from way off somewhere else. Local barber Frank Dalton said that the rangers harassed the local folks just so they would feel like they were earning their Federal dollars.

When we were chased off the Parkway, rather than staying away, we would engage the Rangers in a game of whack-a-mole. Whenever one of us would get chased off the Parkway at one location, another kid would pop right up somewhere else. If accosted by a Ranger, a kid would be certain to profess total ignorance of any policy that might prohibit the selling of chinquapins on the Parkway. In all fairness though, I am sure that a concern for the safety of the kids selling the chinquapins was a part of the issue.

Sometimes, especially on a Sunday, when the rangers were patrolling the area most heavily, we would post lookouts. Usually there would be two lookouts working with a chinquapin hawker or two, with someone posted on a high bank a hundred yards or so in either direction from the location of the hawkers. Fortunately, the rangers drove black Pontiacs in those days, cars that were distinctive enough to be identified from as far away as they could be seen. As soon as a lookout would yell "RANGER," everyone would run down the bank or into the woods and quickly be safely off Parkway land. It got to be kind of a game for us kids, but I don't think it was much of a game for the rangers. We probably could have made almost as much money by selling our chinquapins while stationed somewhere along Highway 58, but that would not have been nearly as much fun.

Those days are gone forever for a number of reasons: For one thing, it probably wouldn't be safe for a kid to be peddling anything on the shoulder of the Blue Ridge Parkway or any other road nowadays. Not only that, I doubt that many kids today would do the amount of work required to gather a few pounds of chinquapins to sell. And do you think that folks today would be willing to buy a tumbler full of strange little nuts held out to passing cars by a strange little nut who was yelling like a nut?

Any observation about the value of the chinquapin that I might make today is but moot commentary. It is now almost certain that the chinquapin, a close relative of the American Chestnut, is also vulnerable to the chestnut blight. The Allegany Chinquapin is on the verge of passing into extinction.

Somebody's Gotta' Do It

Most of the folks I know are truly concerned about the loss of so many of the factory jobs that once drove the economy of this country. Of course, there are also those who claim that there are actually a lot of jobs available, but they are going unfilled, either because they are hard and unpleasant, or because potential employers cannot find applicants who have the level of skill or training that is needed. Then, there is also the claim that a lot of people who are unemployed won't take jobs because they get too many benefits from not working. While there may be some truth in some of these claims, I have talked to a lot of people who lament the loss of the jobs they once had in industries such as furniture or textiles, and many of them even continue to dream of someday getting those jobs back. While none of them talked about how much fun they had while working in a furniture factory or a textile mill, only a few complained about how tough it was.

A situation that was described by some men I know who work for a large dairy farm gives credibility to the claim that there possibly are some unpleasant jobs available that a lot of folks just won't take. The dairy employs a number of workers who work irregular shifts for hourly wages, and there are apparently always jobs available for anyone willing to do a physically demanding and bad smelling job that pays a little over minimum wage and offers few benefits. It is not surprising that some of those who will take the jobs

153

may be immigrants of dubious status who constantly worry about getting in trouble with the Immigration Service.

A college degree is sure no guarantee of a job these days, especially if the degree was earned from an institution of less than sterling reputation. There also can be a problem for a graduate seeking employment if their degree is in a field with a name that gives no clue about what kind of work the degree might qualify them to do. But the name by which a degree program is known can also be misleading. I recently I ran into a young man who graduated from Virginia Tech a couple of years ago who also happens to be the son of a friend of mine. Quite naturally I inquired about what he had been doing with himself since his graduation.

"Oh, I'm working in A.I.," he informed me, displaying a mischievous grin.

"Oh, Artificial Intelligence? That's great!" I guessed that was what he meant, since he had shown a lot of interest in computers when he was in high school, and I was suitably impressed.

"Nope, not that kind of A.I. I'm working in the Artificial Insemination kind of A.I.," he chuckled. "The best job I could find was supervising the sow breeding operation for a big pork producer in North Carolina. That sort of thing is all done artificially nowadays, you know, and I did get my degree in Animal Science."

Well, that sounded kind of interesting to an ol' farm boy like me. I wanted to know more about it, and he was more than happy to tell me. "I do more than just artificially inseminate hogs," he explained. "There's a lot of record keeping involved, and there's even some research and travel that goes with it. The company I work for is always looking to improve the gene pool of

154

their *Sus Domesticus* porcine stock. I travel to hog farms all over the country looking for top quality breeding boars. I don't buy the hogs though, I just buy their sperm. If you'll check on the internet, you'll see that anybody can order hog semen on line for about a hundred dollars a dose. We save a lot of money by breeding our own line of stock and by harvesting the semen from our own animals, but we also put a lot of effort into improving the gene pool and avoiding inbreeding."

"Of course, a lot of my time on the job is spent in smelly hog barns poking around the rear ends of sows in heat. It may not sound like a great job, but I don't mind it. I have interns from NC State working with me some of the time, and they don't mind it either. They had always rather be working out at a farm somewhere than stuck behind a desk or in front of a computer."

The guy's description of his new job reminded me of a time from the distant past, the long-gone days from back when I was still a kid on the farm. I recalled the early 1950's, when a government sponsored project was implemented to improve the quality of livestock on farms across the United States, and it resulted in some previously unheard-of jobs becoming available. The project was administered at the state level by state universities such as Virginia Tech (better known as VPI back then) and at the county level through the Agricultural Extension Agencies. An early indicator that such a project was in operation locally was the appearance of some advertisements in the local newspaper soliciting applicants for some newly available jobs. I think that the first time I ever saw the term "artificial insemination" was when the Agricultural Extension Office put an ad in the local paper announcing that it was looking for an intelligent and hard-working individual to be trained as an Artificial Insemination Technician for the newly created Patrick County Artificial Cattle Breeders Association.

It was reported that twenty-some guys and no women applied for that job. There were not that many good jobs available in Patrick County in 1952, especially government jobs with benefits that included medical insurance and retirement. Another, less common benefit of the A.I. job was the use of a government-owned vehicle, in this case, a bright red Ford F-100 pickup. The association pickup had brightly painted wooden side boards mounted on the truck bed, and foot-high letters on those sideboards announced to the world that the pickup belonged to the PATRICK COUNTY ARTIFICIAL CATTLE BREEDERS ASSOCIATION.

Some of the County's English teachers may have wondered if there was now an association dedicated to breeding artificial cattle, but the dairy farmers in the county all knew what this was all about. There had been articles in the Progressive Farmer Magazine and in widely distributed government flyers that described the plan that the United States Department of Agriculture was introducing to improve the quality of the Nation's livestock. Now, that plan was to be implemented in Patrick County.

There was some opposition, of course. One local dowager of Victorian upbringing realized what the signs on the pickup bed were all about and called the number listed on the sign to complain to the PCACBA. She was concerned that the open display of the signs on the truck was bound to cause young kids to ask embarrassing questions. The County Agricultural Extension Agent who took her complaint on the

156

telephone allowed that most of the kids who would see that sign were farm kids who knew all about that kind of stuff anyway. He also reminded the lady that it was the year 1952, and things like the breeding of cattle were being talked about more openly in this modern age. Had she never heard the use of such terms thoroughbred and purebred? Of course, it was the Patrick County in the 1950's, and there were some ladies who were so prim and proper that they were always careful to refer to bulls as "male cows." "Why don't they just call 'em 'tom cows'?" my dad mused.

In my earliest memories, the breeds of cattle in the little dairy herds owned by folks like us and most of our neighbors (Does five cows even qualify to be called a herd?) was a motley collection of mixed stock in which the specific breed of any individual animal would have been difficult to identify. I think most of the milk cows on the smaller farms in our section of the state were mostly a mixture of Jersey and Guernsey cattle, with a little Holstein and Short Horn sometimes mixed in. The herds owned by the big dairy farms were mostly pure-bred cattle, Holsteins with enough Guernsey animals included to slightly raise the average butterfat content of the milk.

Until then, few of the small farmers had been able to make a serious effort to maintain any purity in the breed of their stock. When buying a young heifer to add to their milking herd, a farmer would usually rely on his own judgment regarding the characteristics of a potentially good milker. If my dad was a typical cow buyer, they were often fooled.

Only a few of the small-time farmers in the area were willing to go to the trouble and risk of maintaining a bull for breeding purposes. Young farm boys such as

157

myself were therefore sometimes given the task of leading a cow in heat to the farm of a neighbor who did keep a bull, a task that certainly contributed to our knowledge about the facts of life. The selection of the bull used to breed a particular heifer was mostly a decision based on convenience, with just enough attention paid to the provenance of the stock to avoid a lot of inbreeding, and the actual pedigree of the bull was rarely much of a factor.

Virginia Polytechnic Institute began to maintain a bank of sperm from high quality dairy animals in the late 1940's, and the Agricultural Extension Service began to offer artificial insemination services to farmers at a reasonable cost just a few years later. Information provided by the AES explained how the quality of most dairy and beef herds could be rapidly improved by raising cattle sired by some of the highest grade bovine stock available anywhere in the nation.

To make the artificial insemination of stock available and affordable, rural Virginia counties organized "artificial breeders" associations. With the help of grants from both state and federal agricultural agencies, these associations were able to provide an artificial insemination service at a cost that even the smallest farm could afford. So when the time came to hire the individual who would carry out the service, there was no shortage of applications, but our neighbor Freddy was the lucky applicant selected to be trained to become the local A.I. Technician.

According to the description, the job first required the successful completion of an intensive two weeks of training in the AI program at Virginia Tech. The technician was not only trained to breed bovine stock, but horses, sheep, and hogs as well. It was, however, the breeding of the improved lines of milk cattle that was expected to be the major boon to farmers in the Appalachian region of Southwest Virginia.

Soon our neighbor Freddy was proudly piloting the fire-engine red Patrick County Artificial Breeders Association Ford Pickup all over the county. We lived right beside Route 58, so we would see Freddy drive by our house in his red truck several times a week. Apparently, a down side of the job was having to work on weekends, since heifers can come into heat any day of the week, even on Sunday.

My dad was pretty enthusiastic over the opportunity to improve our stock provided by this new service, so when our finest mostly Jersey heifer came into heat, he did not hesitate to call the telephone number he had obtained from the sideboard of the PCACBA pickup. The call was answered by the secretary of the County Agricultural Extension Agent in Stuart, and Freddy was dispatched out to our farm to do the deed the very next morning. (You can't wait around too long when a cow is in the mood.)

Before he left for work that morning, my dad gave me definite instructions that when the AI tech showed up, I was to accompany him to the barn to observe and report back to insure that the deed was properly performed. I found this very strange, since I had no earthly idea how the AI was to be carried out. Freddy the A.I. Technician arrived carrying two strange pieces of equipment, one was an object that looked like a trombone case and the other was a metal can which had vapor ominously oozing from around the lid. When the A.I. Technician saw me gawking at the can, he explained that the semen was stored in dry ice. He then instructed me to fetch him a bucket of warm water. I wondered if he was going to wash up the cow.

Once we got to the barn and had the cow secured, the A.I. Tech opened up his case and began to don his A.I. garb, including rubber gloves, one of which came all of the way up his arm and over his shoulder and was secured by a strap that went all the way around his body. The procedure was not anything like I could have imagined. Without my going into all of the disgusting details, just let me explain that the procedure used is called the rectovaginal method in the A.I. business. It involves locating the cervix through wall of the intestine and then introducing the semen via a very long medicine dropper thingy inserted into the expected place. The warm water, as it turned out, was for the A.I. technician to clean himself up afterwards. Throughout the procedure, I kept thinking, "They must really pay this guy a whole lot of money."

A year or so later, I heard that Freddy had abruptly quit his job and joined the Army. A few months after that, I was with a group of guys when we happened to run into him while he was home on furlough, prior to being shipped overseas. The conversation quickly turned to why Freddy had given up his high-paying, draft-exempt job. At first he claimed that his dad needed his help on their dairy farm, but that explanation wasn't sufficient, especially since he had volunteered for the military.

"Did you just get tired of sticking your arm up a cow's butt?" Someone asked the obvious question.

"Nah. I'm an ol' farm boy. Stuff like that don't bother me none," Freddy insisted.

"Did you think they didn't pay enough?"

"The pay was real good. I'll be lucky if I ever find another job that paid as much as that one. It's a government job, you know, and you get insurance, retirement, everything."

"Well then Freddy, why did you quit?" Allen insisted on an answer.

Freddy looked down at the floor. "Well, I just got tired of all the kidding," He lamented. "Being called the County Bull didn't bother me all that much, but I thought guys asking me if there's one kind of cow that I prefer over all the others was just really stupid. Then, when you guys started calling me stuff like *Frednand the Bull* and the *County Cow Frigger*, I decided I just wasn't gonna' take it no more."

We all felt terrible when he told us all that.

Nowadays, I am told, A.I. service can either be provided by a specialist sent out from Virginia Tech, by a veterinarian, or by a guy with a college degree in Animal Science. But most of the few remaining dairies in the state have had their own employees trained to do it all themselves.

Farming looks mighty easy when your plow is a pencil and you're a thousand miles from the corn field.

Dwight D. Eisenhower

Fire One

The men may have looked a little grizzled and tired, but that highway maintenance crew working out of the Smith River Shop had the reputation of being one of the hardest working and most highly productive in the state. But Elmer Hough, the shop superintendent, would tell anyone who would listen that any outstanding performance of this crew was entirely due to his skillful management. According to Elmer, they were really of a bunch of bums who, without his careful supervision, would be a crew of worthless slackers.

The country had been through a lot in the preceding twenty-five years. Americans had struggled through the Great Depression, emerged victorious from Second World War, and most folks were still trying to understand the reasons for the Korean Conflict. The expectations of the American labor force had also gone through a lot of changes during that time, but Elmer Hough's management strategy had not kept up. Jobs were now a lot more plentiful than they had been in the thirties, and a lot of the more recent state hires simply would not tolerate Elmer's condescending attitude for long. By the mid-fifties, the highway maintenance crew at the Virginia Department of Highway's Smith River Shop had separated into two distinct groups. There were the newer and less experienced men, many of whom would request a transfer to another shop

163

following just a short stint under Elmer's supervision, and there was the core group of experienced, older men who were accustomed to effectively working together. They could get the job done in spite of Elmer's interventions, and they could see little reason to request a transfer with just a few years left to retirement. After years of working for Elmer, they had begun to think of themselves as the survivors.

Many of the cohort of long-time employees' had been farmers until the depression had forced them to find some alternative work. Fortunately for them, Roosevelt's "New Deal" had included subsidies for state and local highway projects with the specific objective of providing employment for men precisely in their situation. To someone of Elmer's political bent, the men hired under those conditions were wards of state who should really be replaced with cheaper labor. While they may have been regarded as welfare recipients by their superintendent, there was not one man among them who had not kept body and soul together for most of his life through a combination of hard work and native intelligence.

The standard uniform for highway workmen in those times was exactly the same as what they had worn when they were farming. They all wore blue chambray shirts and bibbed overalls, and almost every head was covered by a felt slouch hat. After a hot day's work, with all of the men's shirts and hat bands darkened by sweat, the highway work crew looked like a cast of characters straight out of a story by Steinbeck. Elmer took care to distinguish himself from the grimy, sweaty men he supervised by always wearing matching khaki work shirts and slacks, meticulously washed and pressed. Sweat stains were seldom ever visible on Elmer's outfits.

The most elderly member of the highway maintenance crew was Tab, a lanky, raw-boned, mountain man, a quiet and watchful individual who was not given to idle chatter. One reason he didn't talk a lot may have been the big chew of tobacco he always kept lodged in his cheek. Whenever Tab took the trouble to spit his to quid out into his palm, clear his throat, and begin to speak with that deep, deep voice of his, experience had taught the rest of the crew that it would be worth their while to give pause to whatever they were doing and listen. Tab's once impressive physical strength had diminished somewhat through the years, but even as he approached retirement age, he earned everything the Highway Department paid him and then some.

The construction foreman, Bennett – never called Ben by his fellow workers – was a man of diverse abilities. Skilled through years of experience as both a farmer and a builder, he was a man with a lot of know-how. He was the true leader for the rest of the crew when they were engaged in demanding projects such as pouring concrete abutments or erecting bridge steel. Bennett was definitely one of the main reasons that the Smith River Shop was one of the most productive in the Virginia DOH System.

Arthur was a large man with a ruddy complexion and a ready sense of humor that helped make working under Elmer more tolerable for everyone else. Always pleasant and good humored, he had a way of making a joke about even the most exasperating situation. Arthur's wry comments, usually delivered so that they were audible to the workmen but not the superintendent, were a common irritation for Elmer. Whenever the men in the work crew were chuckling about something, Elmer correctly assumed that he was the butt of another of Arthur's wry jokes, but there was nothing he could do. When Elmer had complained to the district engineer that Arthur was insubordinate, there was not one other worker who would support his accusation. Elmer's boss knew the real score.

Mac, the mechanic working out of the Smith River Shop, was known for his truck, no pun intended. Because so many equipment repairs had to be made out on the worksites, any time he was not busy repairing and maintaining equipment, Mac was working on improving, organizing, and adjusting the way his mechanics' truck was equipped. The State Department of Highways sometimes had funds available for the upgrading the mechanics' vehicles, but few of the mechanics had used those funds as effectively as Mac. The Reading Service Body installed on Mac's truck was not just equipped with boxes stocked with the standard mechanics' tools, but in the two years since that truck had been assigned to him, Mac had equipped it with both an acetylene gas and an electric welder, a roll-out hydraulic lift, a hydraulic press, an air compressor with an array of pneumatic tools, and an electric generator that could power a lighting system that could turn night to day and drive heavy-duty power tools at the same time. Some even said that if Mac couldn't fix it, it was time for it to be replaced.

The fact was, this older, seasoned highway maintenance crew working out of the Smith River Headquarters functioned so well that the district engineer would sometimes even come by the shop after the completion of a project and complement the crew on a job well done, acknowledging their hard work and dedication. The workers appreciated this gesture, but it did not set well with a superintendent who was always trying to garner the credit for himself. No one could recall having ever heard Elmer congratulate anyone on a job well done.

When a terrific summer thunderstorm caused the North Fork of The Mayo River to flood and wash out the bridge on County Road 640, it created a lengthy detour for a lot of county residents and made replacing that bridge a high priority project. The bridge was one of the few wooden highway bridges still in service in Patrick County, and when the district engineer made the decision to replace the bridge with a newer design made of concrete, it created a niche project, one too small to put up for bids from outside contractors and one [almost] beyond the capability of the local shop. Elmer has insisted to the district engineer, however, that his crew could get the job done in jig time.

There were a lot of heavy storms that summer, causing the construction of the new bridge to get off to a slow start. Twice, right after the coffers for the abutments had been put into place, rain storms had washed them out and filled in the excavations that had been dug for the forms. With summer fading, the only thing accomplished so far had been some site preparation and the placing of the coffers back into the river bed for the third time. Coffers are steel temporary dams used in projects such as this one to keep the water out of a river bed while the foundations are dug and the wooden forms for the abutments are placed and filled with concrete. The water had to be pumped out of the coffers before the forms could be built, and for that task, a dump truck with a large water pump mounted

167

on its lowered tail gate had been backed into place on the river bank right next to the site for the new bridge.

The water pump available to the Smith River Shop was an ungainly military surplus contraption powered by a big old V-4 air-cooled Wisconsin gasoline engine. That type of Wisconsin engine was familiar to many of the workers back then, since they were used to power all kinds of machinery, ranging from hay bailers to fork lifts. They were powerful for their size and well known for their durability, but engines like the one connected to the water pump had no electric starter and they could sometimes be really difficult to start.

On this water pump set up, starting the engine was made even more difficult by the fact that the engine and pump were setting on the tailgate of a truck, putting the engine at about head height. Workers who were experienced in manually starting engines were well aware of the dangers involved in manually cranking a large engine mounted up high like that one. To manually crank that kind of engine, enough leverage had to be applied to the crank to turn the engine crankshaft, while keeping enough distance to avoid being clobbered by the flying crank handle, should the engine happen to backfire and eject it. Unfortunately, this particular model of engine was also famous for its tendency to backfire while being cranked.

Although the coffers had been put back in place the evening before, the crew had not been able to get the pump engine started the following morning. Tab had been trying all morning to crank that engine, and after he was completely winded and had to stop and rest, Bennett took over. Bennett was the one who could usually get contrary equipment like this pump working, but after an hour of futile cranking and adjusting, the engine was still silent. Arthur then took his turn at trying to crank the pump, while also fooling with the choke, the carburetor, and the timing, until the engine probably now had no chance of starting. Then Tab decided to give it another try.

This was a real problem; the work could not proceed until the water had been pumped out from inside the coffers, the morning was getting away, and a convict crew from Horse Pasture was due on the site to start digging out the river bed and placing the forms right after lunch. Tab had just begun his second turn at cranking on the pump when they saw Elmer coming down the road in his orange state pickup.

"The pump is as good as fixed now," noted Arthur. "Here comes Mr. Wizard." All of the workmen were still chuckling as Elmer drove up and parked on the shoulder of the road next to the river. Tab didn't look up, but simply redoubled his efforts at cranking the stubborn pump engine.

Elmer climbed out of his pickup and stood for a long minute, his hands on his hips, clearly displaying disgust as he watched Tab's cranking efforts. When he could stand it no longer, he stumped over to the river bank to see what had been done so far that morning. Elmer was obviously upset when he realized that the entire morning had been spent with three workmen unsuccessfully trying to crank one water pump and the coffers were still full of water, just as they had been the evening before.

Elmer jerked his hat off of his head and threw it on the ground, launching into one of his famous superintendent-from-hell tirades. "You dad-blamed bunch of dumb-bunnies can't get nothin' done. No wonder we stay so far behind. You should have had them coffers pumped out hours ago. I could get more work done with a bunch of old ladies."

Then Elmer focused on Tab, who was still trying to start the pump. "When you crank on them things, you gotta' put some beef into it," Elmer shouted. "You can't just pussy-foot around. Now just get the hell out of the way and let me show you how it's done!"

As Tab backed away from the pump, Elmer walked over to it, spat on his hands and briskly rubbed them together. Then he grasped the crank handle with both hands.

Now, when crank starting an engine of that size, it is a terrible idea to grasp the crank handle with both hands, and it is even worse to crank by pulling down on the handle.

Elmer gave out with a mighty grunt as he swung down on the crank handle with his full weight. The engine responded by backfiring, shooting a flash of fire back through the carburetor, and jerking the crank handle in the reverse direction. Elmer was grasping the crank handle tightly with both hands as it spun backwards and came off of the crankshaft of the engine. As the crank handle flew out from the engine, the socket end swung around Elmer's two-fisted grip, up and over, and coming down on the bridge of Elmer's nose with a loud "thwack." Elmer gave a loud bellow as he threw the crank handle into the air and clutched his injured nose. The poor nose had instantly begun spurting blood.

As Elmer staggered blindly around, holding his nose with both hands and hollering in pain, he stepped off of the bank and fell the three foot distance into the river, striking the water horizontally with a loud splash. The river was only a couple of feet deep there, so Arthur and Bennett slid down the bank into the water and grabbed Elmer, quickly pulling him upright. Tab helped Arthur and Bennett up the riverbank. They all assisted Elmer out of the river as he continued to clutch his unfortunate nose. Arthur helped Elmer lay back on the river bank and Bennett carefully applied a wet bandanna handkerchief across the nose. Bennett said that it looked like Elmer's nose might be broken and that they needed to get him to a doctor right away.

Soon, as Elmer's bellows were reduced to grunts and eventually subsided into sighs, he sat up and again began giving orders while continuing to hold the bandana over his injured nose. Unfortunately, the injury affected Elmer's ability to speak, causing his commands coming out something like this... "Benned, you dake be to the dogtor. "Ardur, go find Magk. Dell hib to ged ober here now and fidz dad dam bump endgine. Dab, you sday here width de bump."

As Bennett and Arthur helped him into the pickup, Elmer suddenly had another thought. He stood up and yelled back over the pickup hood to Tab, "Dab, dond dobody duch dat dam bump 'dell Magk getz id figdz. D'ue hear be?" Tab understood every word.

Mac was out of the shop on another repair job, so it took over an hour for Arthur to track him down and for Mac to pack up and drive back to the bridge. Tab occupied himself during that time by squatting on the river bank, spitting tobacco juice at the water striders in the river.

Mac pulled his truck onto the side of the road near the site, and as he climbed out he asked the obvious. "What's the matter with the pump, Tab?"

" 'Twon't start," was Tab's terse reply.

"Well, when you try to crank it, will it fire at all?" That was Mac's next concern.

Tab walked over to where Mac now stood by the water pump. "It won't fire at all....hardly," rumbled Tab, clearing his throat as he spat his quid of tobacco into the river and placed his hand lovingly on the old Wisconsin engine. "It just won't hardly fire a'tall," he repeated, stroking the cowling of the engine.

"But hello-boys, if this here thing don't never fire again, it hit one dang good lick."

Real Good Stuff

Even before prohibition, a lot of mountain folks had little use for government taxed alcoholic beverages of the type they derisively referred to as "red likker." There is a verse in one of the many versions of the traditional song, *Good Old Mountain Dew* that describes that preference.

> Mr. Roosevelt, told me just how he felt
> On the day that old dry law went through:
> If your likker's too red, it will swell up your head.
> Better stick to that good old mountain dew.

The level of goodness in some of that "good ole mountain dew" is also well illustrated by a Mayberry story that I have heard since I was a kid. The tale is almost certainly apocryphal, but it does illustrate how uncritical some of those mountain folk were when it came to drinking their legendary mountain dew, no matter how awful it actually may have been.

As the story goes, there was this flat-lander who happened to be visiting relatives in the community of Mayberry and decided to go out hiking one Sunday morning. He went walking along a foot trail that led from the Mayberry store all the way to the Pinnacles of Dan, a distance of about three miles. Much of the land through which he would be hiking was quite rugged, and the flatlander was advised that he should take care to stay on the trail. The advice was given not only because of the rugged terrain, but also because he would be hiking through an area in which several illegal stills were known to be located.

Sure enough, just about the time the hiker got within view of the Pinnacles, he met up with a tough-looking local character walking up the trail out of the Dan River Gorge. The local man looked much like a cartoon version of a mountaineer, complete with full beard, bibbed overalls, a battered wide-brim hat, and he was carrying a large stoneware jug. Although the handle of a big revolver was sticking out of an overall pocket, he seemed pretty friendly.

"Howdy stranger," the mountaineer greeted the flatlander. "Nice mornin' ain't it?'

Of course the flatlander agreed that it was indeed a fine morning, and as soon as they had exchanged pleasantries, the mountaineer pulled the corn cob stopper from out of his jug and held the jug out to the stranger. "How about havin' a little swig of Mayberry's finest?" he offered.

The flatlander was skeptical. "Uh, no thank you," he declined. "I hardly ever drink, especially when I'm hiking on a rugged trail like this one."

The mountaineer adopted an angry scowl and pushed the jug up against the stranger's chest. "I said, let's have a drink," he growled, pulling his revolver from his pocket and waving it toward him.

The flatlander immediately declared that he would be honored to sample the contents of the mountaineer's jug. Accepting the jug, he turned it up and took a hefty swig.

"Aggghh," the flatlander coughed, as he lowered the jug and gasped for air. When he finally regained his ability to breathe, the stranger gave the mountaineer a frank opinion of his brew. "That is the worst, the foulest, the most disgusting concoction I have ever tasted," he unloaded on the mountaineer, as he handed the jug back to him.

The mountaineer's scowl turned into a big grin as he accepted the return of his jug. "Well now, ain't that the truth," he agreed, lowering his pistol. "Hit's some awful tastin' stuff alright." Then, grasping his gun by the barrel, he held it out to the stranger.

"Now, stranger," he commanded, "you hold the gun on me."

My own experience with moonshine has been rather limited, but I'll have to say that the best I ever tasted was pretty awful. Even as a kid, I knew it was around, and in my teen years I knew what it meant when I heard one of the older guys whisper that he knew where you could get some real good stuff. It meant that either he had formed a friendship with one of the local moonshiners or that he had been out with one of the girls from down on Troublesome Creek.

The recent proliferation of entrepreneurial distillers who make corn liquor legally and promote it as the modern equivalent of moonshine seemed rather strange to me at first, but I guess it does make sense. White liquor, distributed with little aging or refinement, is the most basic form of alcoholic spirits, and it can be made from a wide variety of raw materials using simple equipment. Simply put, it is cheap and easy to make.

A late great uncle of mine was a moonshiner of some repute, and I would love to be able to hear his reaction if he could see orange or blueberry flavored corn liquor being marketed as "white lightning" and touted as being "the real thing." I heard my uncle talk a bit about the difference between good and bad moonshine, and according to him, the main line of division was whether it was made exclusively from corn or largely made from cheaper alternatives such as Daisy Middling's Hog Feed and table sugar. Sometimes, he said, the addition of a lot of sugar was required to get a batch of mash to ferment, but he and a lot of other folks thought that "sugar-head," as it was called, was definitely an inferior product.

In the region of the Blue Ridge Mountains where I grew up, illegally made white liquor was a commodity which was not at all hard to come by. Nevertheless, a large majority of the people in our mountain community did not drink alcohol to any significant extent. Some who otherwise abstained would drink a morning toddy or a coffee lace, a libation that was almost always taken following a sincere announcement that the booze was being imbibed strictly for its medicinal benefits.

Even my sainted grandmother, a woman who had always fervently wished that she could have marched by the side of Carrie Nation, would occasionally take two tablespoons of rock and rye to relieve her mild angina. This self-medication was always accompanied with a pronouncement of how regretful it was that she had to partake of the devil's brew, but it was the only thing keeping her out of the grave. Otherwise, she would not be found within a mile of the stuff.

Unfortunately, there were also a few folks around who appeared to drink for the express purpose of getting as drunk as possible as quickly as possible, and I suppose those were the hard-core drinkers that the prohibitionists wished to deprive of strong drink. While I was growing up in the mountains though, the nearest thing to social drinking I would ever see would be a group of men behind a building somewhere, furtively passing around a bottle or a fruit jar. This common-but-shadowy occurrence was conducted mostly in the dark outside of social events such as VFW dances and funeral wakes. It was rare that anyone participating in those clandestine communion services drank enough to show any sign at all of intoxication.

Whenever I was close enough to hear the comments of the men who were sharing liquor, it seemed that every one of them felt duty bound to make a positive comment about the quality of the hooch each time he took a swallow. "Whew!" A drinker might exhale, as he would take the jar away from his mouth. "That-there is some really good stuff!" This was a bit confusing, since I had heard that there were some moonshiners somewhere who made really bad liquor, and I even knew that there were people who died from drinking bad moonshine. I do not recall ever hearing a local imbiber say a negative word about the liquor he had just sampled, however. I just assumed that the local moonshiners were exceptionally competent.

There were a few occasions during in my teen years when I had the opportunity to sample some illicit brew. Given such an opportunity, I would usually take a tentative sip just to be sociable, and regardless of my true opinion, I would always imitate my elders by making the declaration of approval that I assumed to be expected. Secretly however, I formed the opinion that white corn liquor was so awful that people only drank it because they were really desiring of alcohol in some form and that the locally made moonshine was the only thing available. I was sure that if they had access to any alternative, they surely would have chosen it.

So here in the twenty-first century, when it is a rarity to find a city or a county which does not allow for the legal distribution of alcoholic beverages, why would anyone buy unaged white corn liquor, even if assured by its makers that it is a true facsimile of the original "Good Ole Mountain Dew?" I am of the opinion that so many people are making legal white liquor these days because it easy to make, and I also guess that the people who make and sell it know very well that most of the folks who might buy it nowadays are unlikely to have ever sampled the original stuff.

Although I was never a fan of moonshine liquor anyway, my low opinion of the stuff was solidified the night some schoolmates and I were celebrating the occasion of our graduation from high school. The girl I was dating at the time was a couple of years younger than me and she was the offspring of some very protective parents. That graduation night, they had emphatically specified that the young lady had to be home by ten-thirty sharp, implying that a graduation night was just the sort of time when young folks were most likely to get into some kind of serious mischief. They were probably right.

There was little enough for a dating couple to do in our rural community anyway. There were two small restaurants where young folks might go for a burger and a coke, but both of them were usually closed down by ten p.m., and there were twenty miles of mountain road that separated our community from the nearest movie theater or skating rink. That particular evening, following the graduation ceremony at the high school, my date and I went to a local restaurant known as

J.O.'s, where we ate hamburgers and played pin ball. Playing pin ball was an activity of which my date's parents would surely have disapproved, had they known, and that definitely made it a lot more fun for both of us. When I took my date home, we sat in the car in her driveway for the allotted five minutes, until her mother began flipping the porch light on and off. After delivering my girlfriend safely home fifteen minutes ahead of curfew, I drove directly from her home to the Parkway Esso Service Center, the epicenter of the Meadows of Dan, Virginia, night life in those days.

The Service Center was closed by eight o'clock on most nights, but that did not mean that nothing ever happened around there after that time. After it was closed, a lot of young guys would gather in their cars at the service station lot. This was the late nineteen fifties, a time when the normal thing for young men to do in the evenings was to group together in their cars, rev their car engines, and talk about cars and girls. Sometimes, mostly on weekends, some of the guys would be accompanied by their girlfriends, as we performed the coming-of-age ritual that was as common in the Blue Ridge Mountains of Virginia as it was in Riverside, California. There were, of course, some fundamental differences. We raced our cars on crooked mountain roads instead of on flat desert freeways, and the beer we occasionally drank had to be secreted in from across the county line.

Typically, when a bunch of guys would drive their cars in for a nocturnal gathering at the service station, they would pull into the lot so that their cars kind of formed a circle around the pump island, with some of the drivers opening car doors to provide a little light. The most common topic of discussion among the guys would have been about who had recently done what to his car engine to get an increase in horsepower. These discussions often resulted in challenges and those challenges meant that every so often, a couple of the cars would peel out of the parking lot and line up side by side for an impromptu drag race down the semi-straight stretch of Highway 58 that ran past the Station.

On this graduation night, however, there was supposed to be something special happening. Word had been spread that an older guy who hung out at the service station, Dudley Wheeler, was going to bring over a half-gallon of his daddy's moonshine to help us celebrate. If you think that a half-gallon of moonshine does not seem like much booze for a graduation celebration, it is probably because you are unaware of the potency of the moonshine and the fact that there were only nine guys in our graduating class. It was assumed that the girls in the class would not be attending the festivities, so a half-gallon of moonshine would probably be more than enough.

Several of us graduates and a cohort of friends had been waiting for some time when Dud finally appeared, driving his hot '57 Chevy Bel Air Coupe. He climbed out of his car cradling a half-gallon canning jar in the crook of his arm like it was a baby. "Anybody want some real good stuff?" he inquired.

As the gang gathered around him, he screwed off the lid and offered the jar to the guy nearest to him. The recipient of the jar held it up so that he could check the level of the liquid in the dim light, then he lifted the jar to his mouth and took a timid sip. "Man, that is really good stuff!" he announced, as soon as he was able to speak.

"Oh hell, man! Dud responded. "You didn't drink enough to even tell if it's any good. Gimme back my 'shine." As soon as the jar was returned to him, he wiped the rim of the jar on his shirt sleeve, then tilted it up and chugged a couple of swallows. Then he held out the jar to the guy on his other side and croaked, "Next?"

The jar moved around the circle and before long it was my turn to partake of our graduation communion. I knew I would be ridiculed if I just took a tentative sip, so I bravely tilted the jar up and chugged what I estimated to be a truly manly swallow. The liquor seriously burned my throat as it went down and arrived at my stomach as an expanding ball of fire. It had an aftertaste that I can only describe as a combination of kerosene and Clorox, but I managed to hold the booze down and affirm to everyone present that indeed it was some real good stuff. Then I passed the jar on to the next guy. Soon, much too soon, the jar came around again and I took another hefty swallow. Whether the jar made its way around to me a third time I am unsure, but one way or another, the contents were soon depleted. That suited me just fine. I was already beginning to feel somewhat woozy and not much later I became seriously nauseated. I wobbled over to the island and steadied myself by holding on to a gasoline pump.

I will spare you most of the unpleasant details, but let me just say that I spent the next hour or two on the pump island, wedged between the high-test and the regular pumps, hanging on to them as though they were my two best buddies. Between the times that I was occupied with heaving out my own innards, I could hear sounds related to a similar activity coming from other locations near the perimeter of the service station lot. I

181

took small comfort in knowing that some other guys were in a condition similar to mine.

Sometime after midnight I managed to make my way home, creep up the stairs, and crawl into my bed. Thank Heaven the next day was a Saturday and I could sleep in until seven. Unfortunately, my bed immediately started spinning, and for the rest of the night I had to keep one foot on the floor to keep it stable. After a pitifully few hours of fitful sleep, I was awakened to begin the morning chores, all performed while nursing a churning stomach and a throbbing head. Although my condition was obvious to my dad, he did not say a word until we were inside of the barn and well into the task of milking. Finally, from the far side of a cow, he cleared his throat and seriously asked me, "How much did you have to drink last night, Son?"

"I didn't have that much to drink, Dad," I told him. "I just took two or three sips from a jar of white liquor." I was being completely truthful. I had taken only two, possibly three swallows, all of which could not have amounted to more than half a cup. I could not understand why it made me so sick.

"Where did you get the likker, Son?"

"Well, Dudley Wheeler brought a half-gallon as a graduation present for us guys, I admitted. "He said it was some of his daddy's best."

"Dud Wheeler? Ain't he L.G. Wheeler's son?" my father pointedly asked.

"I think he is," I told Dad. "Dudley is older than the guys in my class, but he hangs out a lot up at the station. He often has liquor with him, but this was the first time I ever drank any of it. He said that he brought us some real good stuff."

"Lord have mercy Son," Dad scolded. "Everybody knows that L.G. Wheeler makes awful stuff. I wouldn't drink anything L.G. made if somebody held a gun on me. I would have thought you would know better. He doesn't make that stuff to sell it to the folks around here. Most of what he makes gets hauled off down to Myrtle Beach or to Fort Gordon. I'll bet that boy took a jar of L.G.'s liquor without him even knowing about it."

The barn was silent for a few minutes, except for the sounds of the cows chewing and the milk squirting into our buckets, but Dad soon cleared his throat again. Any time my dad cleared his throat in that particular way, it meant that he was preparing to lay forth something he thought especially significant and he expected that I would pay serious attention.

"Well Son, I'm no expert," he began, "but as far as I have been able to tell, there's really only two kinds of white likker. Some of it is "real good stuff," as they call it, but the problem is that a lot of folks who drink are less than honest about whatever it is they are drinking. Sometimes, an honest man would be bound to say something like 'This shit ain't fit to drink' and then maybe even pour it out! Instead, they puff out their chests and declare something like, 'Man, this is some really good stuff.' There are just some folks who consider it downright unmanly to call a spade a spade when it comes to drinking moonshine."

We had finished milking and were walking to the spring house when Dad brought up the subject of moonshine for the last time. "Let me tell you about the two kinds of moonshine," he said. "If it really is good stuff, all that really means is that it is probably not poison, and if you don't drink too much of it, you will probably be able to keep it down. But there is also the bad stuff, likker that just might kill you."

"Now, I've been told that L.G. Wheeler doesn't even drink," he continued, "and there's a saying that you should never buy likker from anybody who doesn't drink his own stuff. But there are still a few folks around who make white likker that is at least safe to drink. I know some folks below the mountain who make moonshine brandy that is safe to drink and even tastes pretty good, but I truly recommend that you not drink hard liquor at all. But if you ever want to try moonshine again, ask me first, so I can at least tell you where you can get something that is <u>safe</u> to drink." My dad never mentioned the incident again, and I never had an occasion to ask him where I could buy some safe moonshine.

A few years later, as a student at Appalachian State University, I was assigned to share a dormitory room with a guy from North Wilkesboro, North Carolina. My new roommate, Tom Trivette, was a few years older than me and was going to graduate school on the GI Bill. He gave the impression of a serious guy who was really focused on his studies, but it turned out that he knew an awful lot about corn liquor. He happened to be, coincidentally I am sure, working on his master's degree in chemistry.

One Sunday evening, as Tom unpacked from a weekend visit to his home just down the mountain, he pulled an enormous Listerine bottle from his overnight bag and plunked it down on the top of his chest of drawers. I didn't think a thing about it until a couple of days later, when, after a long evening of studying, Tom got up from his desk and retrieved the bottle. He tipped his chair back against the wall, screwed the top off the bottle, then turned it up and took a healthy swig. "Whoo-ee," he exhaled.

"Don't tell me that you drink Listerine," I commented, somewhat concerned. I was a fairly serious student myself, and I was beginning to wonder if I had been assigned a wino for a roommate. I had heard of hard-core alcoholics who drank stuff like mouthwash and almond extract, but until that moment, Tom had never displayed behavior that I would have associated with any kind of substance abuse.

Tom gave a good-natured laugh and brought the bottle over to where I sat. Holding the open bottle a few inches from my face he instructed me to "take a sniff." It had been a few years since my last exposure to the stuff, but I recognized the fumes instantly. "Good God man, that's corn liquor!" I exclaimed, pushing the bottle away. I was pretty dismayed, and not just because of my previous moonshine experience. Alcoholic beverages on the ASU campus were strictly prohibited at that time, and the penalty for possession was expulsion. The Town of Boone and all of surrounding Watauga County were described as being as dry as the Mojave Desert in those days. "Are you trying to get us kicked out of school?" I asked.

"Of course not!" he responded, thrusting the Listerine bottle back toward me. "Here, have a drink. It's some real good stuff."

"No thanks, definitely not," I told him as I pushed the bottle away. "I can hardly even stand the smell of moonshine."

Tom returned to his chair, took another sip, then replaced the lid on the bottle. "Are you a Methodist or something?" he asked, "Or do you just not drink?"

"Oh, I don't have any great convictions against the stuff," I assured him. "I'll drink a beer or two once in a while myself. But I had a bad experience with moonshine a few years ago and since then, just the smell of it makes me want to puke. I don't like any kind of hard liquor, and I really can't stand moonshine." Then I explained my concern that the dorm manager might find the booze in our room and we would both be expelled.

"Well, I don't want to get kicked out of school any more than you do," Tom assured me, as he again opened the Listerine bottle and took a small sip, "but I do like having a little hooch available for a nip every now and then. I figure that instead of stashing it in some cranny, the best place to hide your booze is in plain sight. I doubt if anyone ever actually searches these rooms for contraband anyway, but if someone finds it, they'll probably think that it really is Listerine."

"Well, so long as it doesn't get us into trouble, it won't bother me if you drink it," I told Tom. "And you sure won't have to worry about me drinking up your booze. If I am going to drink anything, it is not going to be white corn liquor."

Tom again tipped his chair back against the wall, took another sip, and appeared to seriously thinking for a minute or two. "Well, you are probably right to be suspicious of moonshine," he said thoughtfully. "At least you should be suspicious of just any old moonshine."

Then holding aloft his Listerine bottle, he attested to the quality of his own booze. "I can assure you that this white lightning was not made under a laurel bush somewhere out in the piney woods though. This stuff was made under conditions that would do justice to the finest bourbon distillery in Kentucky."

Tom continued to sit back in his chair, tippling occasionally and being very thoughtful. "Hell, it's all just vodka, really" he said quietly. He must have seen my skeptical expression through his half-closed eyes, because he suddenly sat up straight and stated more emphatically, "It is, man, it really is. All white liquor is pretty much the same as vodka." My roommate then proceeded to give me a detailed lecture on the theory and practice of manufacturing white liquor.

"Sure, there can be a lot of difference in the quality of the stuff," Tom began, "and you are right. Some of it can be really, really bad. There are some old boys who will go on and on and about creating smoothness and flavor in moonshine through their special recipes and distilling techniques, and that is all pretty much bull shit. This is white corn liquor we are talking about, not Calvados. It is intended to be drunk while still unaged and unmellowed, and it is ready for consumption as soon as it has cooled to room temperature." Then he paused for another nip.

"The best you can get is a pure, absolutely clear, mixture that is about fifty percent ethyl alcohol. All the rest is water, just like it is in vodka. It doesn't matter if it is made from corn meal, from cracked corn, from hog feed, or from potato peelings, the result of properly made moonshine is almost identical to vodka. Originally, vodka was made totally from potatoes, but now it's made from grain, just like almost all of the other spirits. But whether you flavor it with juniper berries and call it gin, use some molasses and call it rum, or make it from corn and call it mountain dew, it is still basically the same stuff as vodka."

"When you taste plain white liquor, any flavor other than the burn from the alcohol is a result of impurities and is probably a negative. If the color is anything significantly other than clear, that is a result of either contamination or of over distilling, and that is bad too. If you want red whisky, you have to get into the business of aging it in charred barrels, and that is another consideration altogether. But if you have some bad corn likker you want to improve, you can remove a lot of impurities by letting it age for a couple of months in a crock full of charcoal briquettes, and if you want to pretend its bourbon, let it soak with some oak wood shavings at the same time. I knew some guys who used to make counterfeit Bourbon just that way. And a lot of cheap liquor, especially brandy or rum, has had most of the flavoring added after it was distilled anyway."

"There have always been two fundamental requirements for making safe hooch: sanitary conditions and a lead-free still. Everybody has heard the stories of stills that use automobile radiators for the condenser. They are deadly because car radiators are put together with solder. Solder is mostly lead and antimony and both are poisonous. Heavy metal poisoning used to be a significant hazard for the habitual moonshine drinker."

Tom appeared to be getting a little tipsy, and I think he told me some things that he might not have, had he been completely sober. "It is kind of hard to maintain sanitary conditions if your still is located somewhere in a dirt cave on a creek bank, but I suppose it can be done. Now this stuff here..." Tom again hoisted his Listerine bottle, "was distilled in a building that also houses a commercial bakery. You can't beat that for a location," he grinned. "There you have sanitary conditions, the availability of all of the ingredients; the grain, the sugar, and the yeast, and the smell of the rising dough and the baking bread that covers up the smell of the fermenting mash."

"Another favorite location for making moonshine is on a hog farm. All the ingredients are already there and no one is going to smell the mash fermenting for sure, but sanitation can be a bit of a problem," Tom chuckled.

"One of the main things a good moonshiner does is to cook the mash just right before the fermenting begins. You need to just heat it enough to pasteurize it so that it won't be fermented by bacteria or wild yeast. Sometimes a part of the mash from one run is added to the next one to help get it started fermenting, and that is what makes it a sour mash. It used to be that if a back country moonshiner didn't have enough money to buy yeast, he could always start the mash to fermenting by throwing in a shovelful of horse manure. I've been told that it worked pretty well."

"Ethanol is what you want, but sometimes wild yeast or bacteria can convert some of the cellulose in the grain husks into methanol. Ethanol good, methanol bad, but the methanol can be separated by carefully watching the temperature during distillation. The methanol vaporizes at a lower temperature than ethanol, so it can easily be captured first and discarded. But did you ever see a picture of a moonshine still with a thermometer sticking out of it? Hell no. Moonshiners that make the good stuff will usually just throw away the first little bit that comes off, and that takes care of any methanol. But a lot of moonshiners are not going to throw away anything, especially if they are not going to drink it themselves. Another contaminant is a bunch of stuff generally referred to as "fusil oil," and it gets into the liquor from over distilling, continuing to cook it after the ethanol has all been distilled off and the temperature has gone way up."

"Ethyl alcohol can be made from almost any carbohydrate, anything that falls into the category of fruit, vegetable, or grain. Vodka was originally made from potatoes and rum was made from blackstrap molasses. Brandy is made from fermented fruit, and whisky can be made from corn, wheat, rye, or barley. The product is almost the same, regardless of the raw material, all pretty much ethanol and water. The final product depends more on the technique and temperature used in aging and storing than on what was fermented to make the alcohol in the first place. Folks who make red liquor will sometimes tell you that it's mostly the barrel that determines the quality of the booze."

"Years ago, almost most all white liquor was made from corn, but a lot of moonshine nowadays is mostly made from table sugar. In a lot of operations, as soon as the beer is siphoned off from the mash for distilling, more sugar and yeast is added to the same mash and it is fermented and distilled again and again. The same mash is used for several runs, so it really doesn't matter much if it starts out as corn meal or hog feed. That "sugar head" likker is definitely an inferior product, although it's not quite as bad if it is made from corn sugar instead of table sugar.

"When I say it all is really vodka, I mean that really well-made moonshine is indistinguishable from vodka. I have even thought of buying reagent grade ethanol, diluting it by about half with distilled water, putting it in canning jars and selling it as moonshine. It would be cheap, safe, and hardly anyone would know the difference."

Tom summed up his seminar by telling me that there were really only two kinds of moonshine. The simple mixture of ethanol and water, the "vodka," as he was so fond of calling it, is the "really good stuff," moonshine that is reasonably safe to drink. "The other is not such good stuff," he said, "and that's the stuff that can kill you." Tom the chemist ended his long lecture about moonshine by telling me, in essence, the very same thing that my dad had told me years before.

You take a little trash and you mix it up with ash,

And you throw in the soul of a shoe,

Then you stir it awhile with an old rusty file,

And then call it that good old mountain dew.

Another example of the many, many verses that folks have added to "*That Good Ole Mountain Dew*" over the years.

HAYSTACKS

"Dad, what's a haystack?"

The question from my ten-year-old son caught me by surprise, so I gave him the obvious flippant answer. "Why, a haystack is a stack of hay, Son. What do you think?"

"Aw Dad, I know that," he complained. "But I'm always hearing people say things such as 'Looking for something is like trying to find a needle in a haystack.' I have an idea of what a haystack looks like, but I don't think I have ever actually seen one."

Then the quizzing really began. "How much hay is there in a hay stack? Why would anyone stack hay anyway? Does anyone make haystacks anymore? Is hay just any old tall grass, or does it have to be some special kind of grass?"

At first I was skeptical of my son's claim that he had never seen a haystack, but after thinking about it for a bit, I realized that it being the year of 1978 AD, it must have been nearly twenty years since I had seen a haystack myself. Answering his question was going to be more complicated than I first thought, and I decided the question deserved a serious response.

"It used to be that any old grass that could be cut and stored for use as animal feed was called hay," I told him. "It was often cut from fields that had grown up in just any combination of weeds and wild grass. Some years, the hay would be so bad that we would joke that it might be better for the cows if we just fed them snowballs. But some farmers make a considerable effort to grow and harvest nutritious, high quality hay for their horses and cattle."

"Hay can be a carefully cultivated crop of special grass that is selected because it is known to make good hay. My dad, your grandfather, used to sow both timothy grass and crimson clover seed in our meadows. The first time we cut hay in a summer it would be mostly tall grass, and the second would be mostly clover. Some of the folks we know in Montana actually till the fields and plant special varieties of hay and alfalfa. They even irrigate their hay fields and grow the hay to sell. Their hay is put into great big half-ton bales for hauling long distances. None of them have been putting their hay up in stacks for years."

"How big are haystacks? The haystacks I helped put up when I was about your age must have been about ten feet tall," I told him. "After the hay had been cut and we were getting ready to put it up, Dad would start by picking out a real dry spot in the field, where he would dig a post hole and put a tall wooden pole in it, kind of like a small utility pole, but much lighter. We would lay a few old fence rails or wooden poles on the ground around that tall upright stack pole to keep the hay stack off the ground. After preparing the spot for the stack, we would start bringing up the hay and piling it around the pole. But I'm getting ahead of myself."

"Before we would get into the actual process of putting up a haystack, though, there were a lot of other things that had to be done. First the hay had to be cut, and in my earliest recollections, the hay was cut with a horse drawn sickle mower. Later, it was cut by a sickle mower mounted on a tractor, and before you ask, a sickle mower is a long bar with teeth that move back and forth to cut the hay."

"After the hay was cut, it needed some time to dry. The next day, or even the one after that (if it didn't rain), the hay would be raked into rows, which for some reason are called windrows. Before we could begin to put the hay in a stack, we used pitch forks to put the hay from the windrows into piles about three feet high that we called shocks. After the hay had been shocked, we would slide a pair of slender poles under a shock of hay so two people could carry it to where it was to be stacked. It must have taken about thirty shocks of hay to make a good hay stack. When the shocks were carried up to the stack pole, they would be put in a circle around the pole, just a few feet back from where the haystack was to be put up."

My son's interest in hay stacks had clearly been satisfied, but my memories of the process of getting up hay and stacking it were so strong that I could not help but ramble on. "One worker would pile hay from the shocks up around the stack pole while another would walk around the pole, stomping on the hay, packing it down, and kind of wrapping it around the pole as he went. Packing the hay down as it was placed around the stack pole was called tromping the stack. I began "tromping" haystacks when I was a just little kid, maybe as young as ten, although my dad liked to use a heavier person to tromp the haystack if someone was available. Whomever was "tromping" the haystack had to stay on top of the stack from the time it was started until it was completely built up, walking round and round, hanging on to the pole and "tromping" down the hay with high and heavy steps, packing the hay down as dense as possible. Sometimes those haystacks got quite tall as they neared completion, so the "tromper" had to be careful. As the stack got taller, the "pitcher" would toss the hay up onto the top of stack with an especially long hay fork. The tromper would then have to step on the hay to hold it on the stack as the pitcher withdrew his pitchfork. The tromper's timing was very important; it was easy to get stuck by the pitcher's pitchfork or to let a fork-load of hay that had just been pitched slide back down the stack and onto the pitcher's head."

"Finishing off the stack was the hardest part. The hay would often be piled higher than the top of the pole and the tromper would be handed up a pitchfork to stick into the top of the stack and hold onto. The really scary part was when you were told to use that pitchfork to comb the hay out from the center. Dad wanted the hay on the top of the stack to be smooth, like a thatched roof, so the stack would shed rain. The tromper had to be able to use his pitchfork to keep from falling off the stack at the same time he was combing with it."

"When I was a kid tromping a stack, when the stack was done and all of the pitchforks were moved away, I would slide off the stack and my dad would catch me. That was the only fun part of getting up hay. But after I got too big for that, Dad would help me off the stack by sticking two pitchforks into the side of the stack and holding them, one higher than the other, for me to step down on. He would alternate the positions of the pitchforks down the side of the stack, so I could use them as steps to climb down the side. That was not so much fun. It was kind of scary and I would often get briar scratches from hanging onto the side of the stack.

Hugging a haystack is also a very good way to catch poison ivy."

My son's eyes were glazing over, but I was too deep in my memories to quit talking. "I think a typical haystack back then probably held the equivalent of about a hundred of the small square hay bales," I mused. I topped off my lecture about haystacks by going into the attic and looking in the 1950's World Book Encyclopedia. There was nothing listed under Haystack, but in the section on farming, the encyclopedia had displayed a definitive picture of the classic American haystack. The caption below that picture explained that haystacks were actually a relic from the days in which farming was quite different than it was being done in the modern days of 1950.

"Why don't they make haystacks anymore?" The picture had apparently renewed my son's interest just slightly.

"Well, a haystack is not really waterproof, so lot of the hay goes bad when it is stored in a stack. Some folks were pretty good at putting up a haystack that would shed water like a thatched roof, and that was considered one of the most valuable skills involved in putting up stacks of hay. Of course, when hay is bailed, it is compacted into a smaller volume, so it can be stored indoors efficiently and there is not much spoilage.

"Stacking hay takes a lot of manpower. It takes a team of at least four people to put up hay into stacks with any degree of efficiency, and it must take twelve or fifteen man-hours of labor to put up a good stack of hay. At seventy-five cents an hour, it would cost about ten dollars' worth of manpower alone to put up one haystack, not to mention the horse or tractor time required. Back then, family members did not get paid, of course. At minimum wage today, it would cost over a hundred dollars in labor to put up a stack of hay."

All the information I was sharing with my son was more than he or anyone else would ever want to know about putting up haystacks in this day and age, but he did have one more question. "Did you ever help put up haystacks?" he wanted to know.

"Did I ever put up haystacks!" This was a real "Why, when I was your age..." moment for me. "Do you know that a lot of that land along Highway 58 where your granddad lives was once hay fields? And so was a lot of the land across the road where Mrs. Harris and where Mr. and Mrs. Stanley live. We would put up about a dozen haystacks every summer, before Dad started paying someone to bale it for us. I used to help get up hay for both of my grandpa's, I'd help Mrs. Conner, the widow lady who lived next to us on Route 58, and also I would help Mr. Dehart, Mr. Cockram, and Mr. Burnett. I helped a lot of neighbors get up their hay. I do know a thing or two about putting up haystacks!"

"We might be able to see a real haystack if we went to Amish country somewhere up around Lancaster, Pennsylvania. We ought to drive up there sometime and see if we can find a haystack," I suggested. A few years later we did drive all the way through Western Pennsylvania to upstate New York, but we did not see a single haystack.

*****

More than thirty years after the haystack conversation with my son, my grandson asked one day, completely out of the blue, "Grandpa, what are haystacks?" It was truly a déjà vu moment, but I keep

198

up with the times and this time I was ready with a brand new haystack information plan. But I did take the time to remind him that a haystack was, after all, just a stack of hay.

"Scotty," I said to my grandson, "let's go to the computer and Google *Haystacks*." That is exactly what we did, but the result of our search was somewhat unexpected.

Our Google search revealed some amazing information: it yielded about thirty-five *haystack* cookie recipes and at least half a dozen articles promoting some unusual geological formations called *Haystacks* as desirable tourist destinations. There were three sites that showed how to securely stack square bales of hay, several sites with pictures of nineteenth century paintings of haystacks by famous artists such as Monet and Gauguin, a couple of sites showing photographs of fields filled with modern hay rolls, and a brief biography of a retired professional wrestler by the name of *Haystack Calhoun*. The paintings provided an impressionist view of some haystacks, but the images were really not detailed enough to be useful for anyone who had never actually seen one. I suggested that next maybe we should try Googling either *Amish Haystacks* or *Early American Agriculture.*

Under "Amish Haystacks," we found several photographs of fields filled with shocks or sheaves of either wheat or rye straw, all mistakenly identified as haystacks. From that I learned that there are apparently some photographic journalists who do not even know the difference between hay and straw. Perhaps that difference is strictly academic today, but in the time and place that I was as a lad, anyone who could not distinguish between hay and straw might have been considered somewhat simple minded, so we Googled "Hay vs Straw." This brought up a historical story about the eighteenth century Prussian General, Friedrich Von Steuben, who fought for the colonists in the American Revolution. He was dismayed to find that many of his colonial recruits could not even tell their left from their right. Prussian soldier's boots were lined with straw in lieu of socks, so in order to compensate for the lack of basic knowledge among his troops, the general told his sergeants to stuff hay into the left boot and straw into the right boot of each colonial recruit. The sergeants were then to drill the recruits by marching them around to the commands of 'hay, straw, hay, straw…'.

Scotty and I continued to search Google until, at long last, we did stumble across a series of pictures showing a farmer and his wife putting up a stack of hay. The couple appeared to be using methods very similar to those we used on our farm back in the nineteen forties, the same primitive haying methods that I had attempted to describe to my son so many years ago. The caption below the picture, however, explained that the photographic scenes of the farmer and his wife putting up hay were recently taken near Onesti, Romania. The accompanying article also mentioned that the haying methods displayed in the photographs were still very much in use in that part of the world. The Romanian Lady who was photographed as she was tromping the haystack looked like the ideal person to pack the hay down around the stack pole, since nature had endowed her with well in excess of a hundred kilos of tromping capability. The haystacks put up by the Romanian couple were exceptionally tall and well-constructed, and I could not help but notice that the

Romanian farm couple was using wooden pitchforks similar to some I once saw stored away in my grandfather's barn when I was a kid. Even back then, wooden pitchforks were considered obsolete and were no longer used.

"Grandpa, how does that woman get down off the haystack when it is finished?" my perceptive grandson wanted to know.

"The same way I would get off the top of a haystack when I was a kid," I told him. "She'll just slide down the side of the stack and the farmer will catch her." Scotty looked at me with a quizzical expression and we both burst into laughter as we both imagined the fate of the poor farmer when he attempted to catch his very sturdy wife.

If you are interested in knowing something about real haystacks, stacks that really are stacks of real hay, hay stored using the same methods that have been in use since the days of the Roman Empire, I can save you some time. Just do a Google search for *Romanian Haystacks*.

A Sickle Mower mounted on a Ford 8N

Cornbread Grace

A good friend of mine for many years was an engineer who had emigrated to this country from Hungary following the failed revolution of 1956. He always seemed to appreciate American culture and values, and he was someone whose opinions I valued. I once asked him if there was anything about American culture that had struck him as being especially odd when he first came here. He pondered for only a minute before answering, "Well, I did find it very surprising that people in America eat corn. In Europe, corn is used only as food for animals, not for people."

Although my friend may have been surprised to find that people in the U.S. eat corn, that did not mean he was all that reluctant to eat it himself. One of his favorite American dishes was Texas style chili made with masa and served with cornbread waffles. And although he declared my wife's cornbread to be a culinary marvel, he could never quite bring himself to eat corn on the cob.

I told him if he was surprised that Americans eat corn today, he would have been truly astounded if he had been here a hundred years ago, especially in the southern part of the country. I told him about how my grandmother, who took on the household responsibilities at the age of twelve, claimed to have baked a pone of cornbread every day of her life for seventy-five years following the death of her mother, first for her father and siblings, and later for her own husband and family. My friend responded that he believed corn was not even being grown in Hungary a century ago.

It is a matter of record that corn, much of it in the form of bread, has been the staple food in the rural South and the Midwest from the time those regions were first settled through the much of the twentieth century. In the Appalachian Mountain regions of the South especially, corn was the ubiquitous crop, grown as food for both man and beast. One reason for its importance was that dry cornmeal was one of only a few foods that could be kept for long periods of time without having it spoil in the times before canning and refrigeration. In some of the early chronicles of life in the remote regions of Appalachia, the people there were described as having to eat cornmeal mush every morning and cornbread every evening in the late winter months. Now, after having been considered a joke by urban Americans for years and even falling out of favor even in many rural Southern households, television chefs such as Paula Deen and Paul Prudhomme have made cornbread respectable for everyone once more.

Nowadays, cornbread is being made in an amazing number of different forms. I know this because I just recently Googled cornbread, and over 30 pages of cornbread recipes popped up. Apparently, there is someone, somewhere, who makes cornbread that has just about any condiment you can name added to it. Recipes for cornbread that contain either cracklings or whole grains of fresh corn came as no surprise to me, but I also found recipes for cornbread that is spiced up with everything from jalapeno peppers to mountain oysters. Some of those recipes might be pretty tasty, but there are others that do not appeal to me at all. Can you imagine eating cornbread that contains caviar or maraschino cherries? These aberrant forms of corn pone should not be too surprising, though. We all know about the folks from the northern part of our great land who contribute to their long list of culinary deficiencies by putting sugar in their cornbread.

The thirty-some pages of recipes I refer to included only those recipes for cornbread that is made in the conventional forms of pones, loaves, muffins, or sticks. Recipes for the many other derivatives of cornbread such as hushpuppies, tortillas, and corn flakes, fill many more Google pages.

Another corn-based dish that appears to have gained (or regained) widespread acceptance in recent years is grits, especially when it is served in the form of such trendy dishes such as shrimp and grits. Although grits, sometimes called hominy grits, is often promoted as a ubiquitous southern food, I will have to confess that, although I grew up in the Southern Appalachians, I cannot recall ever sitting at a table where grits was served until after I was eighteen and had moved away from home. Possibly the grits belt begins somewhere to the south of Virginia

There continue to be some remote parts of the country where you may get a snickering response if you even mention the word "corn." This probably indicates that the only use for corn those folks are familiar with is liquid corn, corn in the form of spirits distilled from fermented corn, also known as white corn liquor or moonshine. In fact, one of the many pro-prohibition arguments of the early twentieth century was the claim that much of the precious grain that was needed to provide sustenance for both man and farm animals was being converted into spirits. In the dismal Reconstruction years that followed the Civil War, that claim was really not much of an exaggeration in much of the South, partly because corn is so much more efficiently transported in liquid form. Then there was the probably apocryphal story of the mountaineer who was bitterly complaining that his wife was using up all of their corn meal to make bread and leaving the family without a drop of likker in the house.

Part of the appeal of cornbread is that it is available in so many forms. Cornbread can be made in the form of a round pone cooked in a cast iron skillet and sliced into wedges, or it can be made in the form of a rectangular sheet cake and subdivided into rectangles for serving. It can be a simple bread made just from cornmeal, milk, eggs, baking powder, and shortening, or it can it be all gussied up with corn kernels, chili peppers, and bacon bits. The most basic cornbread possible, however, is simply a paste of cornmeal and water, cooked directly on the top of a wood-fired stove or on the floor of a fireplace. African slaves in the American South sometimes had to cook this simple bread on the blade of a hoe over an open fire in the field. Such thin simple cornbread cakes are still sometimes called "hoecake" or "Johnny cake" in the South, and similar kinds of cornbread are commonly referred to as corn fritters in other parts of the country.

According to my mom, it was corn, mostly in the form of cornbread, that sustained life in the Blue Ridge Mountains from the time of the Civil War up and well into the twentieth century. She was probably right. She may have been a school teacher by profession, but she was also knew a lot about both history and cornbread.

When I was a kid in elementary school, I would get home from school about an hour earlier than my mom, and one of the chores I was assigned to do each weekday was to start the fire in the kitchen range (or the cook stove, as we called it back then). I was supposed to carefully tend the fire and have it ready for Mom to cook supper when she got home. If I did my job well and had the stove at the correct temperature when she arrived, all was well. If I dawdled and got the fire started too late and the heat of the stove was too low, I was in trouble. If I got distracted and let the fire get too hot, that was just as bad. There was no use on blaming a cool stove on wet kindling either. Part of my responsibility was to make sure there was dry kindling available and to be aware of the condition of the cook stove wood and make all of the necessary allowances and adjustments, whatever the conditions.

On weekdays, Mom would come hurrying home from school and in through the back door at about four-thirty, dropping her school papers and coat on top of the washing machine, and blasting into the kitchen while donning her apron. If she was going to make cornbread, which she did about every-other evening, she would begin by plopping a dollop of lard into the cast-iron skillet and putting it into the oven. Then, she would scientifically check the temperature of the wood burning cooking stove by slapping the top of it with the palm of her hand. With her left hand she would scoop up just the right amount of corn meal with her flour sifter, while using her right hand to pull the big mixing bowl out of the Hoosier Cupboard. She never actually sifted the corn meal, by the way. The sifter just happened to be a convenient scoop of the right size.

First came the dry stuff; onto the corn meal in the bowl went a smidgen of baking powder, a dab of baking soda, and a pinch of salt. The dry ingredients were given a quick tumble with the wooden spoon and scraped into a mound with a crater in the middle. An egg was broken and dumped into the crater, and then the mixture was stirred with a wooden spoon as buttermilk was poured into the mix. The pouring always stopped at precisely the right instant.

By then the skillet had been properly preheated and the lard all had melted. Mom would remove the skillet from the oven, lubricate the sides with a quick swirl of the skillet, and pour the remaining melted lard into the batter. After just a minute more of swirling it with the big wooden spoon, the batter would have adopted just the right consistency. With the skillet placed on the top of the hot stove, Mom would pour in the batter, taking care to scrape every last bit from the bowl.

The coup de grace before the skillet of batter was placed into the oven was to cut two lines through the batter with the wooden spoon. The lines were made by chunking the spoon up and down through the batter while dragging it from the front of the skillet to the back and then from the left side of the skillet to the right. This would create an "x" across the surface of the batter that would disappear as the skillet was being placed in the oven.

Although Mom would quickly turn to the preparation of the rest of dinner, I don't remember her ever checking on the bread in the oven before it was ready to take out. She did not need any kind of timer either, because everyone could tell when it was properly done, just from the aroma that filled the house.

Once she had removed the bread from the oven, it took only a slight pry with a table knife to break the pone free from the skillet so it could be turned out onto a plate to cool. Once the brown pone had been inverted into the plate, the "x" that had formerly disappeared from the top of the batter would be clearly visible as two dark intersecting lines in the center of the bottom crust.

I was puzzled by Mom's ritual of cutting the "x" through the corn bread batter and I asked her about it. "Oh, that makes a seam where it is easy to break the bread," she explained. "It's easier to evenly break the pone into halves or quarters along those lines."

That seemed like a logical enough explanation, except for one small problem. From watching folks break the bread, and from trying it myself many times, I concluded that the bread was no easier to break along those lines than it was anywhere else. When I pursued the question further, Mom just tiredly told me that, well, she learned to make cornbread from her mother, and Grandma would always score the batter with the spoon in just that way.

Sometime later, as I was watching my grandmother bake cornbread, I observed that she did indeed use precisely the same techniques as those used by my mom, including the facts that neither of them ever measured out a single ingredient and that both of them scored the batter with the wooden spoon. And when Grandma turned out the pone of cooked bread upside down onto a plate, there was the "x" across the bottom crust, just like the one I would always see in Mom's cornbread. I asked Grandma about it.

"Well honey," she explained, "I can remember my mother doing that to the bread she would bake in the fireplace when I was a little girl. But that's not just an "x," it's also a cross. I call that cross my cornbread grace. When I mark the cornbread before baking it, I know that when I turn it out of the pan, the "x," as you call it, will be there to remind me to be thankful for all the bounty that is ours."

They say you can't take the mountain out of the boy, and that is probably one reason why sometimes I still get such a hunger for Mama's cornbread. I left home almost sixty years ago, and Mama has been gone for over twenty, but through all of these years, whenever I get that craving for cornbread and nothing else will do, I just go into the kitchen and whip up a batch on my own.

It's not the same as Mama's, of course, but it's usually not too bad. The problem is that there are just some essential ingredients that are just no longer available. I can no longer buy stone ground corn meal from W.A. Cockram's Mill, for one thing, and I don't have a wood-fired kitchen range for another. Lately, I have even been reduced to having to use a corn bread mix from the grocery store – there's a couple of brands that aren't too bad – and to using canola oil instead of lard (because of heart problems). There are some fundamentals of cornbread cooking that have remained constant throughout my life, however, and they allow me to still produce some decent cornbread.

One of the cornbread fundamentals that simply cannot be violated is the use of a well-seasoned, pre-heated, cast iron skillet. A dollop of shortening should be placed in the skillet before placing it into the oven while it is being preheating to the required 425 degrees (regardless of the temperature proscribed in the recipe on the bag of cornbread mix). I mix up the batter with a wooden spoon while the skillet preheats. I can't tell you exactly why, but cornbread batter simply cannot be properly stirred with a metal spoon.

After the skillet has been heated to the required temperature and removed from the oven, the melted shortening can be spread up the sides to the rim with a wadded up paper towel (Careful now!) and the batter poured into the hot skillet. All this should be done quickly enough after the skillet has been removed from the oven so that the batter sizzles when it first hits the hot skillet surface. That lets you know that a nice crust is being cooked.

This next part is critical: Using the wooden spoon, cut perpendicular lines through the batter by chunking the spoon up and down as it is moved, first from the handle to the far end of the skillet, and then across the pan from one side to another, so the lines intersect in the middle. The two furrows you have plowed through surface of the batter will quickly disappear.

Now pop the skillet into the oven for twenty-five minutes. After the bread has been removed from the oven, you might just want to set it aside and let it cool for a just minute or two. If the skillet has been properly seasoned, anytime you are ready, you can just give the pone a little nudge with a knife or a spatula, and it will break free. Then you can hold a plate against the top of the pone and turn the plate and the skillet over together. The pone will slip out of the skillet and onto the plate with little effort.

Whenever I turn out the pone of cornbread onto its top and into the plate, I can plainly see the impression of the "x" on the flat, browned, bottom crust. Whether it is called an "x" or a cross, those intersecting lines in the bottom crust of the cornbread always remind me to be truly thankful for the bounty I am about to receive.

Image courtesy of Marker History.Com

Favorite Historical Markers

If someone had told me forty or even thirty years ago, that Meadows of Dan, Laurel fork, and almost every other town or community that lies along the section of United States Route 58 that passes through the mountains of southwestern Virginia would have a four-lane bypass around it, I would have thought they were living in an alternative universe. I don't think anyone was surprised when the larger towns such as Danville and Martinsville were bypassed in the seventies, but a bypass around Meadows of Dan? Who would have thought?

I do appreciate the improved comfort and safety and the savings in time as I travel along the improved sections of road that allow me to drive around, rather than through, towns such as Stuart and Hillsville. But as I whiz past them, I also have a sense of loss, realizing that I no longer feel as much of a connection to those places as I once did. I miss seeing the old familiar homes and businesses, and I even miss seeing some of the familiar commemorative historical markers that I used to notice as I drove along "Old 58."

If you are traveling a long distance on Highway 58, it is likely that you will want to take a break from time to time and maybe even stop to enjoy some of the sights and scenes found along the road. When traveling that road from west to east, however, you might notice that once you are out of the Blue Ridge Mountains and into the Virginia Piedmont, (somewhere between Stuart and Martinsville), telegenic sights and scenes become fewer and farther apart. But even if you are traveling through a region that has a scarcity of scenic panoramas, you can always look at the Virginia Historical Highway Markers.

There is a large number of Commemorative Highway Markers to be found in our fair state, a total of something over 2600, and there are plenty of them to keep you entertained in your drive along Highway 58. Could it be just a coincidence that there's a total of 58 historical markers along U.S. Route 58 between Cumberland Gap and Virginia Beach? You will have to take some of the business routes through the towns and drive over some segments of "Old 58" that have been renamed if you want to view them all, however.

There can be a problem in reading some of these historical markers, actually. The paint has become a bit faded on some of them, and just how much of a historical marker can you make out while traveling past it at 65 miles per hour? It is true that some of the markers are printed in large capital letters, and those are obviously easier to read than the ones that use some smaller lower case letters, but there is always the problem of the limited amount of time one can safely take his eyes off the road while reading a marker. It is obviously a good idea to slow down if one is really interested in reading a marker, and it is even better to pull off onto the side of the road if there is space available. Maybe you should check your rear view mirror before pulling off. If there is an eighteen wheeler loaded with pulp wood following right on your rear bumper, you may wish to just keep moving, possibly making a mental note to stop and read that marker at some future time.

Virginia Historical Markers are made from cast aluminum, with raised black lettering standing out from the silver-colored background. Some of the older signs, including most of the county-line markers ("Z" markers, as they are known) are cast in all capital letters, which limits them to about 50 words. Some of the newer designs of Historical Markers use both lower case and capital letters and the dimensions of the sign are slightly larger, allowing them to display up to about a hundred words, but of course, they are harder to read.

There are no fewer than sixteen county line markers along Highway 58 between Cumberland Gap and Virginia Beach. County line markers, unlike all of the other types of markers, have different inscriptions on their two sides. Located at or near the point at which the highway crosses the boundary between two adjoining counties of Virginia or the boundary between another state and a Virginia county, there is always a historical marker that gives the date the county was founded, the individual for whom it is named, and often describing how the county you are about to enter split off from some other adjacent county or counties. Many or all of the county line markers for a given county have the same text on the sides that face away from the county.

It is likely that there are people who do occasionally stop and read the county line historical markers, although I'll have to admit that I have never actually observed anyone in the act. Possibly, the reason that most of the county line historical markers are just a few words printed in capital letters is so people can read them as they ride past, but one should remember that most of those markers were designed back when the speed limit was 50 miles per hour.

Although I sometimes do read county line historical markers, I really do find it somewhat more interesting to read the markers that provide information about exciting historical events. Not that there is information on any Virginia Historical Marker that is unimportant, but I really had rather read about the European's first contact with the Nottoway Indians in Southampton County, or about George Washington visiting Fort Mayo in Patrick County, than read that Floyd County was created from Montgomery and Franklin Counties in 1831. Some of the more interesting markers, such as the one that tells about Daniel Boone's son being killed by the Shawnee Indians in Lee County, tend to be cast with rather small lettering. Those are the ones you really need to pull off of the road and stop to read. If you don't taking the time to pull off of the highway and carefully read such markers, you might not learn that the first Ruritan Club meeting was held in Holland, Virginia on May 21, 1928.

When a bypass is constructed or the route of the highway is altered, the historical marker usually remains fixed on the old, less traveled route. That makes sense when you consider that the location of the event or the structure commemorated by the marker is usually much closer to the old route than to the newer one. The location of the Taylorsville, A.K.A. Stuart, Virginia, historical marker, for example, is in front of the courthouse and right beside Business 58, the old original route of Highway 58 right through the town, and not somewhere out in the country next to the bypass.

Obviously, I haven't read every one of the Highway 58 Historical Markers, but then there are several of them that that I have stopped to read more than once. I would think that everyone driving into Virginia on Highway 58 from the extreme western tip of the state would want to pull over and read about Cumberland Gap, the trail created by Daniel Boone and once known as the Gateway to the West. That marker gets a lot of viewing, but there are many other important historical markers along United States Highway 58 that have been bypassed and all but forgotten. There is one bypassed historical marker that is especially near and dear to my heart. It is my favorite Virginia Historical Highway Marker, and I would like to tell you about it.

For a brief time back in the early sixties, I was finding it necessary to travel from Bassett, Virginia, to Williamsburg a couple of times every month. I tried several different routes on those trips, but on every route I took, it seemed like I would end up driving on Highway 58 for at least half of the trip. (Well, there was one exception. I once drove all the way from Rocky Mount to Scotland, Virginia on State Route 40, but that is a trip I had rather forget.)

In those days, Highway 58 was just two lanes almost all of the way across the state, and I'll have to say that the trip across piedmont and tidewater Virginia can become kind of dreary after you have travelled it a few times. I don't think there was a bypass around one single municipality on U.S. 58 back then, not around Martinsville nor Danville, and certainly not around South Boston or Emporia. It was a tiresome trip alright, with a lot of slow driving through a lot of small towns, but I did get to know some of the historical locations of southern Virginia pretty well. One of the brighter parts of those trips was when, as I neared the end of my return, I

217

would pass by my favorite Virginia Historical Highway Marker.

These days, heading through Danville from the west on Business 58, the highway crosses what once was Stillhouse Creek, just inside the city limits and a couple of hundred yards from where the creek empties into the Dan River. There, right beside the road on the right, is my favorite marker, the one that commemorates the famous train wreck that happened there over a century ago. At that location there was once a forty foot-high railway trestle spanning Stillhouse Creek, and that was the trestle where the Southern Railways Fast Mail Train, running from Washington to Atlanta, jumped the tracks and became known to history as Old 97. Even today, the song written about that wreck, *The Wreck of Old 97*, is familiar to almost everyone who has an interest in American traditional music.

This commemorative sign marks the site where, on September 7, 1902, Old 97 jumped the tracks that ran across the trestle over Stillhouse Creek, killing 9 people and injuring 7. The deceased included the engineer Steve Broady, and the train's fireman, the conductor, and several mail clerks.

Although I may have a few years behind me, I was not around when the wreck of Old 97 occurred. My mother, however, used to tell me about a conversation she had with a relative of ours who knew quite a bit about the event. One of the reasons why the historical marker commemorating this train wreck has long been of special interest to me is that my mother's cousin, Priscilla Yeatts, was a young girl who was working in the Riverside Cotton Mill in Danville at the time the wreck occurred. I was told that she actually heard the crash, even over the loud noise of the looms in the mill. She said that there were workers in another part of the mill that actually saw the wreck occur, and word soon spread to everyone in the factory that a train had wrecked nearby. At first, the foreman told the workers to remain at their stations until their shift ended, but the mill was evacuated a short time later because the train and the trestle had become engulfed in flames and there was some danger that the mill might catch fire.

Other than the cousin's recollections, everything I know about the wreck of Old 97 comes from the ballad written about it, and there are several contradictory versions of the song. The first and the last verses of the version I first learned go like this:

> They gave him his orders at Monroe, Virginia,
> saying "Steve, you're way behind time.
> This is not Old 38, but it's Old 97,
> you must put her into Spencer on time."

> A telegram came to the Washington Station,
> and this is what it said:
> The brave engineer that drove Old 97
> is lying in Old Danville dead.

"Old 97" was one of the first songs I learned to play on the guitar, and almost every time my dad heard me play or sing it, he would remind me that the tune and a lot of the words of the song were "borrowed" from an older ballad named, *The Ship That Never Returned*.

It seemed like every kid in our elementary school knew the song about Old 97. The boys would go around singing it a lot, and often some of the older guys would chime in with parodies, most of which are unsuitable for inclusion in a book intended for family reading. Of the

219

many parodies of *The Wreck of Old 97*, however, the best known must be *The Man Who Never Returned*, a humorous song about an unfortunate rider stuck on the Boston Subway. It was a really big hit for the Kingston Trio in the 1950's.

It is worth noting that there was another railroad closely associated with Highway 58 in that same part of the state, the train that ran between Danville and Stuart from about 1890 until 1943. The railroad was built by the D&W Railroad Company, and although the initials were supposed to stand for the Danville and Western, the slow and unreliable little railway was usually referred to as the Dick and Willie. The demise of the D&W probably began with the upgrading of State Road 12 between Emporia and Abingdon, followed by the road's later conversion to the paved highway now known as U.S. Route 58. Much of the route of that Old Highway 58 was almost parallel to the tracks of the old D & W Railway between Stuart and Danville. After the paved highway was completed, it was possible to drive the distance between Stuart and Danville in a lot less time than the trip took riding the train, which explains why passenger service was discontinued in 1942. Just a year later the railway between Stuart and Martinsville was completely shut down and the rails taken up and salvaged for the war effort.

There are no historical markers commemorating the Danville and Western Railroad that I could find, but there are a number of signs along Highway 58 that are indirect reminders of that long-gone railway. Today there are signs that indicate the location of unincorporated communities such as Patrick Springs, Stella, Spencer (not the same Spencer mentioned in the Old 97 ballad),

Preston, Kohler, Axton, etc., all of which once were stops along the D&W Railroad.

There are a lot of commemorative historical markers in the state of Virginia, and someone must have visited and photographed every single one of them, given that they are now all posted on the internet. It is possible to read every one of the highway historical markers in the state at your leisure, sitting in front of your computer and without even having to get in your car and go out onto the road. Somehow though, that is just not the same as visiting the location and reading the commemorative marker near the original site.

The Virginia Historical Highway Markers serve as a valuable introduction to much of the State's rich history and provide a stimulus for folks to learn more about it. These markers are an important resource that needs to be maintained and perhaps even expanded. Without access to clear, readable, commemorative historical markers, how will the people of the future even know about such things as the fact that there once was a *Mount Airy, Virginia*?

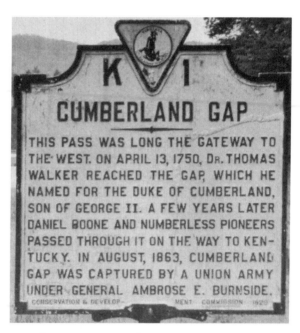

Image courtesy of Marker History.Com

Image courtesy of Marker History.Com

About the Author

Aaron McAlexander is a native of Patrick County, Virginia. He is a retired physicist who now spends a lot of his time in Mayberry, Virginia, mostly writing short stories. Other collections of his stories are *The Last One Leaving Mayberry, So Much to Learn,* and *This Old Store.*

For more information, contact the author at **jamcalex2@gmail.com.**

Made in the USA
Middletown, DE
20 April 2022

64529953R00126